Shaky Relations

EDWARD BLISHEN

Shaky Relations

HAMISH HAMILTON

LONDON

First published in Great Britain 1981
by Hamish Hamilton Ltd
Garden House 57-59 Long Acre London WC2E 9JZ

British Library Cataloguing in Publication Data

Blishen, Edward
  Shaky relations.
  1. Authors, English – 20th century – Biography
  2. Blishen, Edward – Biography
  I. Title
  828′.9′1409   PR6052.L57Z7/

ISBN O–241–10348–7

Typeset by Saildean Ltd., Walton-on-Thames, Surrey.
Printed in Great Britain by
St Edmundsbury Press, Bury St Edmunds, Suffolk.

To my very dear friend
VERONICA MANOUKIAN

We crawled and cried and laughed
Without hope
Without despair.
We grew up
Fenced in by the forest.
But this world of uncles and fathers and mothers and
    others–
Our fine world of greenness and grins was blown away
By the terrible storm of growth...

Mbella Sonne Dipoko: *Autobiography*

Prologue

It was the first day of a rail strike, and I was on my way to see
my father, who was lying ill, perhaps dying—perhaps dead
—in a hospital a hundred miles off, on the south coast.

The sun was shining as I hurried across Waterloo Bridge,
and I caught myself enjoying it—lifting my face towards the
shine of it. There was a sense of some large pleasantness,
coming from that soft, half-wakeful blur of light lying on the
river, and then leaping off it. The sense of leaping came
perhaps from the movement of the surface of the water.
Perhaps it also came from light being caught, thrown up and
lost by the metal of cars. The big buildings·were shining
solids, planted alongside the heavy, winking shake of water.
There was the flow of the river, and the rootedness of the city:
and it was lovely—the association of what flowed, and had
this ever-changing surface, and what was fixed.

I thought: but how can I be enjoying this bright morning,
which might be his morning of final darkness? I was hurrying,
alive, towards his gasping death. I was hurrying through his
London; and for him, at this moment, all place, geography
entire, was perhaps being expunged. I was hurrying towards
my father's annihilation.

But it was wonderful, to breathe in the shining air!

Waterloo was strangely empty: there was no certainty of a
train. I bought a ticket, and fumed up and down the
concourse, feeling oddly like my father. He'd so often been
angry in railway stations. There'd been delay, perhaps, or
insufficient civility on the part of a porter or ticket clerk.
When I was very small, I was excited by the idea I had of
him, as a scourge of slackness ... and not only in railway
stations. He'd been particularly hostile to cinema ushers:

1

never willing to accept the seat offered. 'It won't do them any harm to take a little trouble and find the seat I want.'

A strike, like this one, would cause him to snort with a kind of bitter triumph. It always was like this—slackness, indifference! Even the matter of his ... going to Heaven was subject to obstruction by the unwillingness of workmen ever to work.

Going to Heaven! It was often his phrase for the unbelievable business of his death. The childishness of it made it the bitterest of all his euphemisms. The phrase had a naive shine about it that made its effect, in my father's disgusted voice, all the angrier.

A train dawdled in: seemed willing and ready eventually to depart: was going where I needed to go. I thought, as it made its way too slowly south, how the last two or three years had been full of the decline and fall of relatives. My wife Kate's mother and father already vanished: uncles and aunts gone and going. So many visits to hospitals. My parents had vowed that neither would allow the other to be borne off, again, into those aching, terrified and terrifying corridors and wards. There'd been too many of these experiences of exile from all the precious ordinariness of life. But there'd been that phone call, last night, from my father's doctor. He had to go into hospital, and urgently. It had begun as one of those turns of his, as Mother called them, when waste matter forced itself violently out through his mouth and nose. He'd cried, for himself but also because it was so awful for her. He'd always been the cleanest of men: and had, he often said, been drawn to her, more than sixty years before, by her wholesomeness. They had polished and tidied their lives together, it had been perhaps their only shared passion, and now it was all so disgusting, such grubbiness and disorder in and out!

And it became worse: a refusal of every ordinary function. He'd proposed, the doctor told me, that my mother should go into a nursing home while he was away. But she wasn't a woman for nursing homes, the doctor protested: and rang me. Kate and I said we'd go down and fetch her, at once. And, almost immediately after the doctor had rung off, my father rang.

His usual abrasive voice. He could be very cold, cruel on the phone. It was how our last and worst quarrel had started. Now he said, 'What did the doctor tell you?' Only that he

2

wanted him to go into hospital for observation, I said. My father's snort. 'I'm no fool. You don't go into a surgical ward for observation.' 'You'll be all right,' I said. 'I'm sure. Try not to worry.' His snort this time was withering. 'Good luck, my dear,' I cried, hoping to get it in before the familiar sound of his hanging up.

In the end—because I had work to do at the BBC next morning—my sister had gone down to be with my mother: who said anyway she'd rather stay at home and be near him. Kate and I arranged to relieve her in a couple of days. But, before I could begin work that morning at Bush House, there'd been a phone call. He was unconscious: the proposed —and, I gathered, desperate—operation was not possible. Come at once.

Decline and fall of so much. A generation—the generation ahead of us. It meant—and I had this ridiculous military vision—that Kate and I and all our friends were now in the front line. And for me, lately, there'd been the collapse of my connection with Africa, and the new African writing. I couldn't help smiling, but wryly, at the memory of the accusation that had been levelled at me. I was one of the 'Western flatterers' who surrounded 'Westernised African writers'. It was a curious experience, having such a shrilly polemical phrase suddenly hung round my neck: being transformed between one day and the next into a caricature.

I'd always had an infuriating tendency to approve of any criticism directed at me. I attributed this to childhood reading: having then been appalled by those characters in books who tried to brush aside the only too patently just charges levelled against them. But this was one charge that even I was not ready to accept. If I'd flattered African writers, then I'd flattered hundreds of children I'd taught: my wife, my sons, oh, lots of people I'd met. Because the charge was really one of making encouraging noises. I thought the making of such noises was a basic human duty. It should be accompanied by an effort to discern and articulate the truth, even the painful truth: but encouragement should be the atmosphere in which all this took place.

Well, my father had always provided the opposite atmosphere: one of furious discouragement. If my critic had wanted Westernised African writers (it meant they'd been published

3

in London or New York) to be subject to Western detractors, he could well have started with my father. He was congenitally given to censure. I thought how oddly entwined, anyway, had been, in recent years, that African experience of mine, and the final, baffling struggles that arose from being my father's son, and his being, so often to his despair, his son's father.

At Southampton I asked a taxi-driver to take me to what I imagined must be called the General Hospital. Well, there was such a place, he said, but since I spoke uncertainly he must say there was also the Royal South Hants. They were equally important. I felt, not for the first time, at the mercy of a simple possibility I'd astonishingly failed to consider. It was now obvious to me that a great city might have two hospitals. How had I lived so long before coming to this simple understanding? I chose, miserably certain I'd made the wrong choice, to be driven to the General. I was indeed wrong. There was no ward of the name I asked for. They rang their rival for me. Yes, he was there.

We sped back across the city. 'My father,' I said, hurrying into the ward, 'is ill here.' I gave my name. Ah, would I wait outside? Well, not actually outside. Perhaps I would sit for a moment in this office inside the ward. Someone walked delicately across and shut the door. There were clearly things to be discussed that I shouldn't hear. It must mean he was in a bad way. Then a nurse came in and shut the door again behind her—everything that occurred was an announcement behind which my understanding limped. She asked, 'Do you know anything that has happened to your father this morning?'

'No,' I said.

'Then,' she said, 'I'm sorry to have to tell you that he died an hour ago.'

And my head snapped—cracked—my neck—it was as if it meant to fly off my spine. It was as if I'd been given a karate chop from behind. It was the most unbelievable thing I'd ever heard. It was plain nonsense, to which (as I thought this) I was already adjusting. The feeling was a dreadfully interesting one, of being appalled and of making room for this emotion. He was, I realised, in that tent of screens in the middle of the ward. That's why they'd hurried me into this room.

4

And the great official kindness of the place began to operate. I was taken to another room: urged to smoke: given coffee. Would I like to see him, the ward sister asked. Oh yes, I said. Well, she'd advise against that. Remember him as he was, alive. I gave in; and immediately felt I'd made a mistake. Bad enough not to have got there to hold his hand. Agonised though his dead face might be, I ought to have been a witness to it. Otherwise he'd vanish unacknowledged: and that might have been his worst nightmare. But these feelings were sluggish: I was still in the grip of ... Well, it wouldn't do simply to call it shock. It was the deepest sort of disbelief. How could a father die?

A young doctor. My father, he said, had seemed reasonable enough, was ready for the operation—someone had been talking to him, he'd been perfectly coherent: a couple of minutes later he was deeply unconscious, and never recovered. A coroner's case. Very sorry. Surprising, really.

And I felt grateful for all this considerateness, and at the same time impatient with it. It wasn't a considerate occasion, really. There ought to be something fierce in the air, the sound of huge disintegrations. Instead, there I was in a cab, going to join my mother and my sister, with this paper carrier and my father's typically elegant soft bag, for taking to hospital: both filled with awful odds and ends, his immaculate handkerchief, his toothbrush and his razor, his dressing-gown; and the top, but not the bottom, of the pyjamas in which he'd died.

I went to the house next door, first, and handed in the carrier, the bag. I'd come for them later. Mustn't let my mother see these pathetic objects. I had time to think how horrified my father would have been, to see his final debris handed like this to a neighbour. Of all people, a *neighbour!*

I went in then to my mother's agonised embrace.

My sister said the phone had rung and my mother had stood at her side, mouth hanging open with fear. Betty had listened and said foolishly, 'Well, thank you very much,' and then, to my mother: 'It's Dad ... ' My mother uttered, Betty said, the most extraordinary cry of agony she'd heard—burst into wild tears—clung to Betty—and then suddenly (she'd been preparing lunch) mumbled, 'I must strain the custard.'

And in the midst of her grief, which was raw and terrible,

as if her tears were blood, she asked me where his clothes were, and handkerchiefs, and dressing-gown. And when I said I'd left them next door, she was astonished.

It was among the first things she'd wanted to do: to make a reassuring inventory of the immaculate laundry he'd taken into hospital with him. To take him into her embrace again, in the beloved form of his underwear, toiletry, all the carefully chosen accessories that were of his very essence.

PART ONE

1

'My God,' said my father. 'You *are* looking old.'

He sounded very satisfied. Nowadays, when we went to see him, he made no secret of searching for signs of decay in his son. Some change in general outline, a few more grey hairs, yet another wrinkle—such things made his day. And at once unmade it. That I showed signs of being not a whit more immortal than himself pleased him. It helped him to endure the awful things that were happening to his own handsome body. He also felt it was a fitting punishment, in my case: it might make me a little less eager to parade myself as a bloody intellectual. But at the same time he feared it—my ageing —and his own pleasure in it. In the last resort, it meant we were all falling hideously and frighteningly to pieces together. No comfort in that.

I knew how he felt about it, I suppose, because, cast by life as his most intimate foe, I was also bound to him by ironical resemblances. At certain moments, from inside myself, I caught my face becoming his. His voice threatened to take over from mine. I grinned at him now, as we stood in the kitchen of his ... what was the phrase? ... retirement bunga-low. If I grinned, I could chase some of the resemblances away. Then I looked (if my inside judgement was correct) more like my mother: who was dancing at my elbow, elaborately introducing me to my own father. 'Doesn't he look well?' she demanded, referring to me: and clearly having failed to hear my father's remark. 'Depends,' said my father, with his harsh cackle, 'what you mean by well.' He turned to Kate, who anticipated him. 'All right,' she said. 'I'm looking ghastly, I suppose.' It was a cue for my father to be smooth, deadly. 'Oh, I don't know,' he said. 'That's overdoing it, I think. A bit.' He laughed with bitter joviality.

9

There was an exchange of horrified kisses—in the case of my father and myself, a handshake. We hadn't kissed for forty years.

On the way down, Kate and I had flirted, as we often did, with the fantasy that I had a welcoming father. 'Suppose,' said Kate, 'he was very nice to us. Warm. Pleased we'd come.' We laughed, wistfully. 'I have to remind you,' I said, 'that it's not the easiest thing actually to get into the place.'

That was true—unless my mother was on the watch. Well, she always *was* on the watch. When we were expected, we had to her some of the quality of the United States Cavalry, relieving a besieged outpost. She'd stand, when she could, at the front window, peering in the direction in which we'd come. The trouble was that she'd also be preparing one of her splendid meals. Mother associated the arrival of loved ones with instant nourishment of her own providing. With her, always, food and love had gone together. She'd married my father in order to stuff him with marvellous food till death … cut off the gas. The odds were that we'd arrive at some moment when she was ensuring that the custard was no common custard, but the creamy wonder of which she'd always been capable. She wouldn't be at the window.

Then—as had happened that morning—we'd find ourselves at a seaside bungalow that had the air of a domestic Fort Knox. My father would have latched back the gates: not so much welcomingly, I'd think, as because he didn't trust me to latch them back correctly myself. Given the proper season, the great roses would be blooming in their obedient squads to one side or other of the lawn: which would have had its usual short back and sides. And the problem of the locked doors would face us.

Even expecting visitors, a sufficiently unfamiliar situation, my parents could fail to hear a bell. There was a side bell and a front bell. Neither, though efficient enough as bells went, could be depended upon to command the attention of the inmates of the bungalow. Kate had arrived once on—of all, in my father's view, horrifying occasions—a surprise visit. She had rung fore and aft, she had rattled some of the complex chainwork with which my father kept hawkers, canvassers, communists and mortality at bay, but she had not gained entry till she'd gone in despair to the bungalow next door and

10

phoned through to my parents. My father had been enormously sulky about that: it was a dreadful thing, to involve his neighbours. It gave them apparent grounds for intimate comment. Indeed, Kate had handed him over, bound hand and foot, to those most awful of enemies, the people next door.

So you rang, and banged, feeling substantially foolish—because you were, after all, the next-of-kin, and expected: and all this boltedness and barredness did amount to a species of rejection. But then something would have penetrated, because back along a great vista of barriers you'd hear keys being inserted, locks in operation, latches drawn, a slow glissando of openings: and at last you'd be face to face with your father.

Who would say: 'My God. You *are* looking old.'

My parents had moved to New Chilton on his retirement at the end of the 1950s from the Civil Service. 'We think,' my father had said, in that manner that seemed to make him his own official spokesman, 'the South Coast will be right for us. Sea air. No hills for your mother. Nice properties. We think we might live to a ripe old age in a place like that.' He gave a dangerous bark of laughter. 'Suits us.' You were being warned not to express any of the absurd ideas you were certainly harbouring about this or that element of inappropriateness in the plan.

The nice properties, as it turned out, were bungalows. New Chilton, my father's preferred place of retirement, was overwhelmed by these: all new, all occupied by the retired. If one imagines a visitor entering the place and, out of honest ignorance, asking: 'What is a bungalow?', then the sheer quantity of such housing to be found there might have provided a reply dangerously rich. His mind might have been turned. I was always glad, entering New Chilton myself, to have been prepared in advance for bungalows.

My father had the profoundest scorn for many of the prevailing varieties, and for much that had been done to or with them by their owners. He walked about the place, tut-tutting, mocking: driven to harsh barks of laughter by certain kinds of roofing, certain dispositions of room ('Want

11

their heads examined—kitchen in the front!'), certain species of ironwork ('Makes the place look like a parrot-house!'). He was fierce in some show-houses ('Damned silly place to put a window!'), cautiously appreciative in others ('We quite like the doors'). He developed strong tastes and distastes in the matter of porches, side entrances, sites. Altogether, it was a field day—no, several field months—for that side of him that had always enjoyed looking caustically into half-finished houses.

Then he made his choice.

There'd been a nervous day when Kate and I were taken to see the bungalow chosen. 'What do you think of these?' my father said, as we walked round the town, and some new stretch or close of bungalows came into view. 'Ah,' we said, knowing my father and so wary of any clear comment. It would be like him to try to catch us out, praising what he'd spurned or sneering at what, after that long anguish of consideration, he'd chosen. Luckily, I was an expert—well, after nearly forty years I had better have been—in the fine shades of dissimulation in his voice. It became an exercise in listening very carefully to the faintest of undertones. I also watched, of course, my tell-tale mother. I'd guarded against many a moment of melodrama by keeping an eye on her helplessly blatant face. She'd never, in any case, had any liking for my father's habit of turning the imparting of ordinary information into a nerve-racking quiz. Putting all the evidence together, I was able to say at the right moment, 'Ah, now these are the best we've seen.' 'And that one?' demanded my father, being suddenly, touchingly specific. 'The best of the best,' I said. I already hated its particular tame pinkness. 'That's the one,' my mother exploded. 'It's Daddy's! It's what Daddy—!' As always, my father chose the moment of mother's over-excitement (which so often rested on her delight in some small triumph of his) to be cool and distant. 'No need to shout about it,' he said. 'But we think it's exactly what we want.'

Which it wasn't. Any more than New Chilton was.

I never shook off my feeling of the immense sadness of New Chilton. Lots, one had to say, of dull couples went, while the man was still working, on holidays to this dolefully suburban-

12

ised stretch of the south coast. It was extraordinary to think it had once been on the edge of Hardy's country. Tess of the D'Urbervilles had committed her murder not many miles away. Not *terribly* long before, Englishmen had peered from the local Martello towers across at the Napoleonic rim of France. Now, it was one long villa politely staring out at the, on the whole, rather impolite sea. There'd been, among people native to the suburbs of London, an enormous feeling of the suitability of their going, once working lives were over, to this region in which the surburban fantasy (all that ironwork my father so sturdily detested) and the seaside fantasy were wedded. They went, and found themselves in the grimmest of antechambers to oblivion.

New Chilton was an enormous waiting room. There was a door leading off the waiting room, and the name on the door was DEATH.

My father's excellent, conscientious doctor Mackenzie had written about it, in the local newspaper. How he and his colleagues found themselves serving a geriatric suburb. How as a consequence they were infernally busy, ushering patients through that door. Only 'ushering' was not the word. These exits were usually, for patient and doctor, extremely exhausting. Dr Mackenzie thought that a few healthy youngsters, or almost as healthy middle-aged persons, scattered about in New Chilton's population, might make things less onerous for everyone. There might be, at any rate, some closer resemblance to a normal community: that's to say, one of which a high proportion was not constantly expiring on the edge of a sea that to some was in itself—or seemed to be—fatal.

The devil of it was that the sea had drawn my parents; and they made, when it came to it, very little use of it. My father even came to think of it as a nuisance—being a source of salt that interfered with his gardening, and ruined his paintwork: and a source also of seagulls, given to massive excretions held in until they were flying over his roof. The sea, moreover, made draughts, ultimately murderous in intent ('Nasty wind off the sea—coming straight up Beach Road—we stay indoors till it's stopped'), and munched away at the uninteresting cliff, making it difficult to create the normal appearance of a seaside: the New Chilton beaches being more like half-drowned battlefields. 'Do you know how much of the rates we

13

pay goes to trying to do something about that damned erosion!' It was not now so much the English Channel, which had drawn them to the spot, as the English Eroder. We'd walk along the cliff, carefully, on windless afternoons when we were visiting, but my father's affection for the element was plainly on the wane.

But then all the natural phenomena he'd loved were letting him down. I'd never known such a man for the sun—he'd always soaked it up hungrily: as a younger man had positively confided himself to the summer as to some sort of frying-pan, had lain down in it and browned and sizzled. He'd gleamed, darkly baked, through the summers of my childhood. His delight was to go into the garden early, and leave it late. I think he knew every crumb of soil. Very plainly he was a gardener, from green fingers to green feet. (The way he stepped in a garden had a husbanding air about it. You felt plants might grow where he trod.) I remember him anguishing over asters, enormously uneasy about pinks: and made happy beyond words by chrysanthemums, obeying some subtle law of their existence. They had, mysteriously, no more, no less than the right number of buds.

It had always been absurd that he was a civil servant.

But the sun had become an enemy. It caused dizziness and exhaustion: it was part of a system productive of dangerous changes of temperature. It brought about, or might bring about, colds: which in the nature of New Chilton were the first steps to galloping death. 'We avoid too much of anything.' He still went into the garden, but most carefully, and only after discussion and consultation ('Your mother won't let me out unless she's sure it's safe'—but in such matters she'd always known how to be his confirmatory echo): often, nowadays, in a trilby hat, even in a waistcoat. I hated the severance of my father from what had always been the best things in his life, even though I'd had reservations about the military severity of his lawns, the regimental orderliness of his roses. Everything bloomed under orders— but it bloomed!—and he loved to be the cause of that.

He had become, largely and bewilderedly, an indoors creature, being angry—on the whole—with what appeared on television. He referred now to this occupation of his—we'd hardly had time to sit down, were being conducted through

14

the growling overture to the day's exchanges. In the opening moments of such a meeting he set out to nettle and needle. So now he was expressing cautious approval of certain television programmes in order to bring out differences of taste between us that never failed to give him his special, scowling pleasure. 'You watch—?' and he named some serial. 'Surely!'

'No, Dad. What's that?' He gave his incredulous bark of a laugh. 'My God, you miss everything. It comes after Crisscross Quiz on Tuesdays.' Knowing the drift, I tried not to declare myself about Crisscross Quiz. 'Oh yes.' But his eye was on me like that of some inflamed detective. 'You don't watch Crisscross Quiz either!' 'Well—' He was torn, then, between furious pleasure in finding that I was as I'd ever been, the child deprived of a taste for obvious enjoyments (largely by education, that bloody grammar school)—and the other conviction, that I really *did* watch such things as Crisscross Quiz. Kate and I sat furtively watching them, like half your bloody intellectuals, and then pretended we didn't.

'My God, what a boring life you lead!' he said. I wondered where he'd move next, in this phase of welcoming flagellation. Probably my involvement with Africa ...

Much of his furious approach to other people, I reflected —his compulsive animosity—was now exercised from the armchair where he was sitting: the chair itself, even empty, had taken on a crouching, aggressive look. In the absence of flesh-and-blood persons, anyone appearing on the television screen became the subject of his habit of scorn, with very rare intervals of approval. It was a matter simply of a new sort of neighbours. It was seldom possible in his presence to follow a programme because of the flow of his contempt, irony, distaste or tendency to make references, not always accurate, to the private lives of his unwitting victims. 'That man wants to leave other people's wives alone!' he'd snort, as a newsreader spoke of grave events in the Middle East. 'We can't stand him!' he'd cry, as an interviewer launched his first question. 'Oh my God! Can you tell me why he makes a face like that?' *'There's* a man who cares for appearances!'—another newsreader, the doyen of them all, and in the select line of public figures my father had approved of over the years for their conservative attention to dress and the management of their hair: George Arliss, Ronald Colman, Clive Brook. I'd reflect

15

that if this newsreader were to announce the end of the world, my father would confine his comment to a word about his tie. 'Some of the ties the others wear! Cut out of old curtains!'

At the opposite end of things ... any Labour politician. At the sight of one he'd laugh with noisy meaningfulness, as if the man's very existence was a joke generally understood. 'Oh my God! Look at him!'

A whole range of coarseness was brought out by the appearance on the screen of any but the skinniest of young women. 'Mind you don't lose them, dear!' he'd cry at the least bouncing of breasts. Any young woman laughing would trigger off another jovial apprehension of his. 'She'll wet herself in a minute!' Guffaws, which my mother would dutifully echo.

But I think the worst of it was televised cricket. Towards the end of his life, much of my father's balefulness was turned on the Australian team. I'd sat with him the previous summer watching a test match. His running commentary, blotting out television's own, was shaped by his view of the Australians as such a set of unsporting, near-villainous characters as never before composed a cricket team. He despised their bowlers for showing enthusiasm or hope ('Fling up your arms, then!'), and for smiling ('Watch it! He's got something dirty up his sleeve!') and for not smiling ('They don't know how to enjoy a game!'). He suspected them of having lip salve on their foreheads which they transferred to the ball under the pretence of making legitimate use of their own sweat ('He can't be sweating! The sun isn't even shining!'). He despised their failures and poured contempt on their successes. He mocked the way their bowlers ran up, and condemned a ball that was not hit as a waste of everybody's time by the bowler ('Oh—give him something to play a stroke at!') ...

But now, as I'd expected, he was saying: 'So—you're going to Africa ... Well! Those little black dictators ... They make us laugh, you know. Little whatever-his-name-is! We enjoy their antics ...'

My mother said, 'Oh don't talk politics, Dick! Ted and Kate didn't come to talk politics—'

'I'm not talking politics,' said my father. 'You can't call

16

that politics ... Funny little what's-the-other-fellow's-name?'
He laughed with enormous intent to give offence. 'Where
are you going in Africa, then?'

2

I was going to East Africa, to take part in Book Weeks being
held there. It was a consequence of my being involved,
through the BBC, with African writing.

Eight years before, in 1959, I'd stopped being a properly
employed person—well, a teacher—and had become a freelance writer. People said how brave that was. Fantastic nerve
for a man with a family! But it wasn't so, at all. Teaching and
writing are simply, both, engrossing labours. Do the two
together for long, and it becomes apparent that there isn't
enough of you to go round. I think I might all the same have
gone on for some time shredding myself finer and finer (or
perhaps it would have been coarser and coarser), had not the
branch of teaching I was hanging on to suddenly snapped.
What happened was that the rough secondary modern I'd
been part of for ten years was scheduled for transformation
—in general by what they called reorganisation, in particular
by a new headmaster—into something strange and smooth.
The intention to bring about smoothness was awfully apparent, and I had no wish to be part of it. The old rough
quality of the place could be exhausting, and at worst rather
horrible, but it revolved round a core of honest vigour.
Attempts at improvement should build on that vigour.
The transformed school, I suspected, under the leader-
ship proposed, would revolve round a core of ... preten-
tious langour: which, being not at all in the spirit of the
district, would rapidly become something very unhappy
indeed.

A friend in the BBC said, 'Would you like, as part of your

desperate parcel of freelance labours, to present a programme for African writers?'

Even to say I was ignorant of African writing would not cover the case. I think I had not considered the possibility of its existence. I was directed, by my BBC friend, to recently published work—all by Nigerians. Thus thinly prepared, I waited to receive the first poems and short stories addressed to the programme. I would choose, each month, a story, or some poems: and talk about the choice, in a gently critical way, with readings.

The first story that arrived, I remember, began: 'There were once two tight friends ... ' I was in, though I didn't instantly realise it, with a bang. Among other things, I was faced at once with a fundamental critical question. Did it make sense to say that the phrase, 'two tight friends', was *wrong*? Ludicrously *incorrect*? Misleading, too, since it could mean the friends were drunk? Should I claim there was only one acceptable way of phrasing this, and that was to say: 'There were once two close friends ... '? Please do not vary idioms; and if you are aiming at a cliché, arrange without fail to hit the target.

But wasn't 'tight' a physically expressive word, bringing to life the idea of an embrace, as 'close' had ceased to do?

There were great pedestrian qualities, actually, to begin with—alongside these amazements. Many of the scripts were marked by a simple tremendous desire to make the gestures that, clearly, a story ought to make. So within half a dozen sentences a character would be gasping, pondering, having his heart pierced and his mind heavily weighed upon: accepting the inevitable: looking bemused. His lips squirmed: he nodded to himself: he looked glum and sad. He thundered: he moaned: he uttered a whisper. 'You are a piece of beauty,' he informed his companion: glaring sideways at her as he did so. 'Your lips are firm,' he added. 'They portray an extraordinarily strong and determined nature—yet they are inviting and tempting.' This was part of a general obsessive particularity about the way people were constructed. 'Her hips balanced delicately on a pair of symmetrical and slightly bowed legs.' She had, frankly, an oblong bottom: on this, in pursuit of the hero, she bounced round the room. She spoke: he collapsed—an effect due, it seemed, to her combination of

18

charm of appearance and keen intellect. To round it all off, he decorated his mouth with a cigarette and looked vertically at the ceiling.

There were stories with sad, but inadequately sad, titles. For example: 'One of those accidents in life.' Okpara's and Ada's happy home was broken up when their excellent father was involved in a case of embezzlement: both their parents then died at once: Okpara and his sister were brought up by different people: the fact that they were related was lost to public knowledge through the simultaneous death of all the foster parents: the unsuspecting couple then not only met but fell in love, and not only fell in love but got themselves married: the priest officiating at the wedding knew the truth but for some reason—or, indeed, no reason at all—refrained from acquainting them with it until the ceremony was over: whereupon the ill-fated pair and assorted bystanders were afflicted by that tendency to die in groups that had been the fate of others unfortunate enough to be characters in this story. The title seemed in serious need of revision. It should have read, perhaps: 'Groups of people who have important knowledge of one another should either pass that knowledge on, without delay, or take all practical steps to avoid sudden simultaneous death ... '

Because English studies in the schools never got beyond 1850, much of the poetry that arrived in the early days was couched in a parody of the language of the English romantics. It was clearly difficult to write convincingly about Africa in terms and tones designed for the Lake District. There was a pervasive scent of daffodils—quite the wrong flower. It was in West Africa that this sad burlesque was first brought to an end, by fierce young poets who decided they had a literature of their own to appeal to. It had been an oral literature, absolutely local.

And then *that* excitement had travelled across to East Africa ...

I was on a busy edge of it all, fascinated and confused. There was the humdrum work, which I liked, of advising writers of whom most had little gift, but great earnestness. I was much moved, simply as a writer, by that strong desire to have a story done—or a poem. Maybe it was only a nod in the direction of being a certain sort of person. You wrote a

19

story or two, your dozen poems, as part of a particular pattern of development. I was touched, as it happened, by the idea of literature being thought a necessary step in anyone's growth. But rarely was it possible to say that behind any story, any poem, lay *that*, and nothing more: the impulse to contribute to the school magazine. There was, I thought, even in the least gifted work, a sense of writing as a natural response to astonishing circumstance. Here was Africa being transformed, from day to startled day, and here were people wanting to mark this mysterious excitement of change by writing stories or poems. It seemed to me to establish afresh the elementary function of all literature. You wrote a story, or a poem, however bad, because you wanted to give a shape to events, and to share with others an emerging sense of the way things were going.

You worked blindly, perhaps, even ineptly, but you were part of a human activity of which the total effect was likely to be important and benign.

And there was, besides, good writing by any standards, by a handful of plainly gifted novelists and poets.

Altogether I was full of a paper Africa, and longing to see, smell, hear Africa itself.

3

'Well,' said my father. It was to be one of those visits when he was determined to touch all the sore places. My mother's anxiety was shared painfully between a cake whose splendid genesis she was supervising, and her dread of what he might say. 'These black people ... D'you know—I keep thinking back to when I was young. We didn't have all the do-gooders you have around now. All that social welfare lot.' He laughed at the very idea of such a combination of words: social welfare. Ha! 'There was no such thing in my day. And there was none of this violence then, either.'

Apart from the rest of what he'd forgotten of life in Edwardian London, I remembered stories of his youth in a family of brothers: always full of flying furniture. 'Then Will threw a chair at him.' Once it had been a knife—that was Uncle Jack. 'Terrible temper—my brother Jack.'

Good Lord, yes. If ever there'd been violent people, it was that angry band of brothers. Their very marriages seemed to breed potential carnage. Well, as a child I'd been fascinated by the curious information that filtered down. For example, that Auntie Hilda, who was always passionately leaving Uncle Will and then passionately returning to him, was given to pursuing him round the house with a carving knife. The aim, it seemed, was to ensure that he loved no one but her. For a long time I assumed that her intention was murder. Oddly, whenever I met my aunt, who had an excited pretty face and a habit of pouncing on people and kissing and caressing them—even small nephews—I could never think of her as a killer. It took years for me to appreciate that that had not been the threat.

Passion, synonymous with violent intentions, seemed very much what happened to uncles and aunts. They lived lives of incredible marital danger. It was murmured of Uncle George that his wife would tire him out every morning, so that (as I understood it) he could go on during the day to tire out no one else. I'd overheard my father, raucously secret, discussing this situation with my mother. 'Tire him out! I don't know how she thinks she can tire George out in ... what would it be? ... ten minutes?' 'Dick!' 'Well, how long d'you think she'd have? Quarter of an hour?' It was one of those obscenely precise questions of my father's that my mother refused to answer. They were, of course, designed to bring about the embarrassment of that refusal. 'If she started early ... say, six o'clock?' 'Dick!'

I had a vague image of Uncle George being made to run round the bedroom, and given other exhausting exercises familiar to me from the school gymnasium ...

'And how,' I asked my father now, 'do black people fit into this?'

'I hoped you might ask that.' His laugh, addressed to some accomplice on the ceiling. 'It's obvious. They don't understand how we live. We like a quiet life. Polite, if you like.

21

That's not their way. Well, they can do things however they like. But let them go and shout their heads off and bang their drums and knife each other in Africa—or the West Indies. Not here. This is not the place for it.'

'*Polite* life?' It was only ten minutes since my father had told me how he'd broken off a branch of his neighbour's laburnum that happened to be overhanging his fence, and thrown it into the centre of the next-door lawn.

But he was briskly moving on to other kinds of conversational half-Nelson. This time it was Kate who was his victim. Quicker to lose her temper than I was to lose mine, she took care to spend this vicious opening phase of a visit with my mother: but ill-luck brought her into the room at this moment. My father said:

'Saw what's-his-name ... the chap who couldn't bear living in Russia ... *Nureyev* on television the other night. Looked in need of a bath—*and* a haircut.' Kate whipped round furiously, and he raised the level of his voice. 'I'm only saying it *looked to me* as if he needed a bath.' He laughed rather horribly. Kate ran from the room. 'They're grubby, you see,' said my father. I thought of saying something about the endless showering that was inevitable in the life of a dancer, and even about the unsuitability for most roles in ballet of short back and sides, but decided—as it seemed often sensible to decide—not to take up the challenge. Take up all my father's challenges, and you'd be dead within an hour of arriving at the bungalow.

Oh, that bungalow! It was a little prison that he'd found to lock himself into and other people out of. He would sit at times close to the window and inspect the world of his neighbours, venomously. 'Look at him,' he'd say, as some elderly person passed along the pavement. 'The managing director. That's what he says he was. Couldn't manage my arse.' 'Oh Dick!' my mother would say. As long as I could remember, my mother had been saying: 'Oh Dick!' For sixty years, by then, ever since they'd met as little more than children in the West London slums, she'd been registering her mild, sad protest at his misanthropy. It provided my father with a sort of springboard: he could use her protest to take off into even more vehement sournesses. 'If he was managing director of anything, then I'm the Prince of Wales. As for that stupid little wife of his—' 'Oh Dick!' 'Not that I care what sort of people they are. Doesn't interest me. But next time we meet them in the town I don't want to stand chinwagging with them for half an hour. I'll tip my hat and that's enough.' 'You've got to be nice to neighbours.' Was that mother's millionth attempt to turn her fondness for people into an imperative to which he must yield? Her millionth failure. 'Sod the neighbours. If you'll pardon my French. Why the hell should I be nice to people just because they live next door?'

But his chief attacks were directed at widows. The grounds of this dislike, obvious though undeclared, were that in the nature of things they had survived their husbands. He was possessed by barely controllable rage when he thought of being survived by anyone whatever. Widows, he said, all became plumper, happier-looking, with their husbands gone. They gave themselves airs. They positively *spent* the money that had been left to them. You received the impression, from his angry talk, of a considerable conspiracy of bereavement.

'I hope,' he'd said during one of our visits, 'that I shan't be the first to go. I don't like to think of your mother having to fend for herself.'

'Oh you don't have to worry,' said my mother, perfectly matter-of-fact. 'I should get on all right. I can look after myself. That's the way I was brought up. You ought to know.' She allowed his solicitude to cause her a little indignation, laced with fairly half-hearted gratitude. To which, brightening, she added a new thought. 'I'd *remember* you,' she said. 'I'd be here remembering you.'

She was being practical, not at all unkind. She had never thought it sensible to wish to die. She would certainly miss him, but would be consoled by this function of remembrance.

But not remotely was it the kind of future my father had in mind. He snorted with what was obviously a most complex dismay.

He was worried now about what was happening to him. It came out bit by bit as we prepared to go to a local hotel for lunch. He couldn't breathe at night. My mother described it—his panic-stricken gasps and desperate gulpings of air.

'Poor man.' She giggled as she said it—seizing, as she'd always done, on amusement as a means of making endurable the great amounts of pity he demanded of her, and which she readily provided. Poor mother! torn between a sense of his absurdity, and a genuine sorrow for every ache he suffered! 'I don't worry about it very much,' he said, ignoring her giggle, which meant that he was moving towards the second, mellow phase of the visit. 'I'm better off than some.' Then he gestured towards the window, making reference to all his neighbours. 'You know—some of these people's hearts are too strong. All the rest of them is sick, but their hearts are too strong and they can't die.' He spoke as if he was complaining of overhanging branches of laburnum: but I knew it was what he brooded on most, beyond that dimension of things in which he found neighbours impossible, people who lived lives perversely different from his own. He was horrified at once by the ease with which death operated, and the difficulty of dying. He was altogether tormented by the idea of extinction. 'When I'm a bit of dust,' he'd say: believing with only too appalled an intensity that this was what he would be, without believing it at all.

In the warmth of the hotel bar, he was like a very cramped bud slowly opening. He enjoyed the mechanical exchanges involved in choosing and ordering drinks. 'The same as usual, Dad?' Enormous joviality in his nod: or in his pretence of difficult decision, his slow, grinning: 'Yes, I think I will.' The head waiter would appear from the direction of the restaurant, bearing menus. Towards him, my father had an uncomfortable cluster of attitudes he'd always had in respect of waiters: chiefly, awe, distrust, and a frustrated longing to be aloof and peremptory. What it often amounted to was that he'd make some gruff, challenging confession of ignorance: which, as usual with him, seemed to transfer to the other person any shortcoming that might be involved. This, in a New Forest hotel catering for devotees of plain Englishness, was largely a matter of wines. 'Which of these is sweet?' 'Well, sir—' 'Because I can't tell the difference between them, you know.' Loud laugh, full of implications about the personalities of those who *could* distinguish one wine from another. My mother might say, in one of her ringing whispers, 'Ask Ted!'

24

'Oh yes, I could always ask my son—or my daughter-in-law. They're connoisseurs. Wine with every meal.' 'No, Dad,' I'd murmur. 'But I'd like to ask this *gentleman*. He probably knows even more about it than Ted.' (A delivery of the word 'gentleman' that my father never recognised to be deeply insulting. His habit of being rude to people as a simple mechanical precaution often got him into trouble.) I'd avoid the waiter's sardonic eye. Then, shortcircuiting the whole pantomime: 'What about a Sauterne?'

It was always, in the end, a Sauterne. Another aspect, I think, of his pleasure in these visits: being presented with a choice, and coming always to the same familiar decision. We'd tried, early on, to interest him in other wines: he was politely disappointed in them all. They had a defect which he defined as dryness: a term he added to the rest of the vocabulary in which he discussed our way of life, as he imagined it. We were as guilty of pretending to enjoy dryness as of feigning delight in classical music, the loftier sorts of entertainment provided by BBC television, and so on. Snobs, both.

4

When my father mellowed, he became cheeky. There he was, that afternoon, standing on a ridge of pebbles, close to the sea, in the soldier's pose he'd fallen into all his life. Now it was a stout soldier, trying to reduce the effects of his growing stomach—his breath held in. There was a great cockiness about him. All smell of tobacco it had been once, square brisk hands, refusal of doubt or any carefulness of thought or observation. Instead, at best, this bright, strutting confidence. It was the sunny side of his terrible inflexibility. As a child I'd loved the cheeky bully in my father.

His being in such spirits had made my mother excited and

25

verbally vague. 'Look at his corporal,' she exclaimed: her word always for 'corporation', which, if she'd got it right, would have been her word always for 'stomach'. She was telling Kate how she'd amazed the butcher with her kindness, making do with the wrong joint though it was his fault that it was wrong. 'It'll do just as well as the other,' she'd said. 'He went down on his hands and knees to me,' she added, overdoing it—as so often she did. She was fond of this notion of people collapsing with gratitude in response to simple acts of hers. 'Kate,' she'd remembered over lunch, 'nearly broke down when she came to the bungalow for the first time and found what hot water there was to bath in.' (It was one of the few things she shared with my father—a belief that their life was studded with uniqueness. You could never hope to modify his conviction that even fine weather was a peculiarity of New Chilton.) My brother-in-law on a recent visit, mother averred, had nearly fainted when he tasted the local greens. People—postmen, tradesmen, policemen, bus conductors —were inclined to take her in their arms ('He couldn't make too much fuss of me') and tell her what a sweet little woman she was. Sometimes, from her accounts, she'd hardly been able to get through the High Street for the quantity of these embraces and emotional displays of admiration. There was also praise for her legs as she walked from shop to shop. Amazingly nice legs for a woman of her age, had been the chorus.

She had sensibly, I used to think, elected to pay herself the compliments my father had no habit of paying her.

Back in the bungalow, in his crouching armchair (if ever a chair might spring, this was it), my father drifted again towards sharpness. He'd always been given to tedious fits of moralising. It had never in his life, I think, occurred to him that most matters are discussable and give rise to different opinions. His model of man did not include the allowability of debate. To thought itself, which might lead to complexity of outlook, he set sharp limits. 'I don't let myself think as far as that,' he'd always said, as if declaring some admirable austerity. So at this moment he was not canvassing questions of morality so much as laying down several of his familiar laws in that region. 'It is not unusual,' he was saying, 'for most people at some time during their lives to attach too

26

much importance to the area below the navel.' He had done so himself, it seemed, at some very remote period. My mother didn't appear to think it was all that distant. For years she had taken advantage of his Great War-wounded ear (a drum shattered) to make comments on his more reckless assertions. 'You've never given it up, mate,' she murmured.

'It's happened even to you,' he barked, frowning in my direction. 'Of course,' I said. 'Except that I'm not sure what you mean by *too much* importance. And it does seem a pity to confine it to one half of the body. Or to suggest that it ever comes to an end.' He snorted at the absurdity of such views. 'You worry about your boys,' he informed me. 'You wonder what they're up to.'

It was another characteristic of his: never to inquire how you actually felt about anything, your sons or any other matter. His habit was to tell you what you felt. 'You and Catherine worry yourselves sick sometimes. You can't tell me you don't.'

I could easily and truthfully tell him we didn't—not *sick*: but wondered if it was worth doing so. 'Young Thomas,' he said. 'You're not telling me that you're not worried to death about what he'll get up to at university.'

It was always 'Thomas'—never 'Tom': just as it was always 'Catherine,' never 'Kate'. It was one of my father's devices for keeping people at bay. He wasn't going to be caught going in for the casual warmth of familiar names. It would have been like wearing trousers without creases. An offence against his religion of dapperness. Dapper and distant—that was the thing to be. Even in the family circle, I'd had to come to terms with the dressed-up character he could give to my fond name. He could make 'Teddy' sound quite bitterly formal. Sometimes when, at the rarest of moments, he called me 'Ted' with a companionable intonation, I'd feel close to tears.

'Delighted he's going to university,' I said. 'Can't think why we should worry about it. We hope he gets up to lots of things.' I wasn't quick enough, though. Kate, who at times had small patience with the oblique approach to my father, had cried, *'Rubbish!'* 'Catherine says it's rubbish,' observed my father, like a fielder who'd taken an easy catch. 'I hope she won't look back and feel sorry for saying that. One thing that amuses your mother and me—you thought I was a rotten father—'

'Oh come,' I said.

'But we see you going through the same things that we did—and finding out what it's like.' He turned towards my mother, who with her own growing deafness had only the vague idea that he was being typically unpleasant. 'They'll learn, my dear,' he said, consoling her. Refusing consolation, she cried, 'They don't want to talk about that.' It was a comment that covered many such moments, even when she was unsure of the actual topic of conversation.

'Oh, for goodness' sake,' said Kate. 'We're happy about our sons. We're happy—can't you understand this?—that there's a new life opening for Tom at university. What a dreadful thing—to sit here worrying about *that*. It would take those—Wise Men of Gotham, was it?—who sat crying because someone might fall in the pond—you'd have to be someone like that to sit about with a long face because your son, *hurrah,* was going to a university.'

My father sat stiff and expressionless during this speech: allowed a silence after it, as though giving someone a chance to sneak away after a disgraceful act: and said:

'You don't believe any of that. Now, take Daniel ... '

Daniel, barely recognisable under this formal title, was our younger son Dan. But we were, on this occasion, not to take him. 'How dare you tell me what I believe!' Kate cried. 'You can't shout me down,' said my father: not the first time he'd suggested that Kate might be about to embark on this difficult enterprise. Mother said, 'Now Dick, stop it!' Then, to me, 'What he needs is a tantaliser.' 'Put my foot in it again, I suppose,' said my father, 'To keep him quiet,' said Mother. 'A tranquilliser,' I guessed. My father laughed diabolically. 'I was just being candid,' he said. 'No harm in that.' 'I think I'll make tea,' said my mother. 'And I'll help you,' said Kate. 'I'd like to hear what you've got to say when the boy's been at that place for a year,' cried my father. He laughed for the benefit of a large audience of sympathisers, seated in their usual position, tier upon tier, to one side of the television set. 'I suppose I'll never learn,' he said. 'People don't know how to take me.' 'I can make a suggestion,' Kate murmured, and followed my mother out of the room.

It felt like a suddenly deserted battlefield. My father cleared his throat noisily and glared for a while at the wall. Then he said, 'I expect you'll take this wrong … But I don't think Catherine will make old bones. She gets worked up too easily, you know—it's not good for anyone. Wears them out before their time.'

And there was always a sense in which my father, so misanthropically wrong about things, was also damnably right about them. Of course, simply having children was a cause of nervousness. And of course, having created them in circumstances that might over-simply be summed up as heedless, one was bound to be jumpily heedful of them ever after. Certainly there were times when we were deeply worried about our sons—even at the Wise Men of Gotham level. They *might* fall in one of life's many unfenced ponds and drown. But my father's dark gift was to see the worry, only. It was related to his inability ever to escape from the habit of discovering the meanest and most desolate reasons for any piece of behaviour. Tom going to university didn't appear to him at all in the light of Tom enjoying and extending himself intellectually, emotionally, amorously; it would mean rather that he'd be drawn to unspeakable political opinion; would abandon the last shreds of attachment to respectable clothing; and would sleep with other men's daughters.

It was the idea my father had always pressed upon me from the time of my earliest adolescence, when he clearly imagined that I might at any moment dash out and insist on sexual intercourse with some unfortunate passer-by 'Remember,' he'd say, with urgency, 'that any girl is somebody else's daughter. It's what I always tried to remember when I was young.' It was an occasion for one of my mother's snorts, carefully pitched below the level of his hearing. Inexperienced though I was when first presented with this advice, it seemed to me to lack plausibility. It wasn't easy to imagine young men setting limits to their thoughts about daughters by thinking instead about fathers.

And the truth is that though my father might just possibly have tried to quench his own lustful fires with this particular extinguisher, he'd clearly not succeeded. He had a famous and exhausting record of attachment to other women than my mother. Tom would have been hard put to it, at university or elsewhere, to exceed his grandfather in this respect. The curious thing—and I'd felt the oppression of it very strongly, as a boy—was that the force of his sexuality was matched only by the dreadful negative power of his official puritanism. I could have taken, as a boy, my father's delight in sex, if he'd been able to confess it, far more easily than the morbid and often cruel prudery to which he laid claim. It had led him to distort delight itself, hideously. 'All women are the same when the light's out,' I'd hear him say, when I was a child.

And even now, any attractive woman—a neighbour, briefly tolerated, a tradeswoman—was bound, at some early point in his acquaintance with her, to qualify for excitable condemnations that had little to do with her character, and much to do with his inability to cope with the desires she roused in him. They grew more awful and enraged, I guess, those desires, as the trim younger man turned into the stout older one. In severe cases, he would ascribe to a woman a sick form of his own longings, and hint that she was helplessly loose. A vast amount of folklore, including the compost deposited by centuries of passionate crime, fed this view: which saw a woman as someone who 'led a man on'. It was another of the phrases of my childhood: *'She led him on.'* And sometimes, horrified, I'd see this or that harmless woman through my father's eyes—unable to avoid being Eve: doomed to tempt, with infinitely cunning variations on the apple, all the unlucky Adams within reach.

It would make me think fiercely that a sexually more open society certainly put people at risk: that there were those who battened on openness, and made a business of it: but that there'd been more terrible people still who'd battened on the old secretiveness—on my father's world in which sexuality had been a terrible salty reality, wholly denied and disowned. How much, I'd think, having known both worlds, I preferred the open risk to the closed one ...

30

5

We'd come, now, through the worst part of the commando course that a visit to my father resembled. It was the moment—that arrived on each of these occasions—when, with everyone stinging and sore, I realised he was glad we were there.

It was never anything but a nervous strain to be with him. Kate at times would turn actually white. He could leave no statement of anyone's unshaken—would take any small remark and hang it on the line like a carpet and beat it remorselessly. No avenue was too trivial for him to explore. He couldn't bear you to have anything to say for what you had or preferred, if it was not what he had or preferred. His refusal of the ordinary give and take of discussion, and his perpetual suspicion that a simple remark concealed some more elaborate one, were deeply exhausting. He looked under every statement for its real meaning, never able to accept that people might speak in, as it were, the clear. 'Hmm!' he would say. Enormous disbelief expressed as a noisy clearing of the nostrils.

He had the television on now, and was quarrelling with that. Then he asked if there was anything we'd like to see ourselves. It was the precise moment when I recognised that he was pleased by our being there. I said I'd noticed from the *Radio Times* that a pianist was playing a brief programme of Chopin on the other side. He switched over but at once turned the sound down to a whisper, and was scathing about the fit of the pianist's evening dress. A nocturne was shouted down (I put it to myself, secretly) by a discussion, conducted by my father with himself, of the circumstances in which a white tie should be worn rather than a black one.

It was a relief when he turned back to a variety show. I

31

noticed how, whenever a new performer appeared, my mother would look up from her knitting and cry 'Bless her!' or 'Bless him!' It was as if she was making up for whatever my father might have to say about them.

We'd had a private word, she and I, in the kitchen. He'd been very awkward lately, she said: wouldn't let her accept an invitation to morning coffee from neighbours. 'I'd like to have gone. But he thinks we'd have to have them back.'

Well, yes. But it was deeper than that. He'd talked at lunch about a neighbour who kept his wife secluded for fear of what she'd give away about their affairs. 'He's afraid of her nattering.' He couldn't have been more afraid than my father was of my mother's runaway tongue . . . . It had been a cardinal feature of the world as I'd known it when I was a child: the view that any family was a storehouse of secrets, and that the vital function of the family was to keep those secrets to itself. Everyone was standing guard over vast numbers of dark cupboards.

She'd worked out, my mother said under the sound of a boiling kettle, an idea about the amount of talking people did. There ought to be some restriction on it. 'People would spend a lot of time thinking: then they could use up their ration of talking. For the rest of the time they'd ... relax.' I saw my mother's undeclared vision: of my father, his very small daily allowance exhausted, lying back in an armchair that had stopped crouching, and had become relaxed itself ...

But he was suddenly his better self again. He mocked me for the orange socks I was wearing: it had always been a belief of his that colourfulness of socks was the first step towards moral breakdown. But it was cheerful mockery: and he remained in high spirits when my mother told a confused flat story about something that had happened to her—or, as it turned out, had refrained from happening to her—while she was shopping. 'The excitement's killing me!' cried my father at one point. That was a joke that went back years, too. I'd sit among my uncles and aunts, all of them for once at their noisy precarious best, and my heart would leap with love as my father interrupted a dull story with that same cry.

He was even amiable when, just before we left, my mother

asked, 'You're going to give Ted a drink?' I don't know if he'd have offered something at this point without her prodding. But long ago our family had fallen into unconfessed halves: my father and sister on one hand, my mother and myself on the other. 'Your mother says her blue-eyed boy looked very tired,' he'd say in a letter following up one of these visits. 'We think you and Catherine take life too seriously. You shouldn't be afraid of having a little fun.' And so on. It was because I was my mother's blue-eyed boy that the convention arose that she must press him to give me a farewell drink. She must do this simply to illustrate the point: I was *her* son, primarily. Years before I'd had a passion for rum. Mother built legends out of such things: 'Ted loves rum. He knows he can always have some when he comes to visit us. There's always rum in the cupboard for him.' Or, in her excessive mood: 'Ted nearly bursts into tears when we tell him to pour himself some rum.' One would think the bungalow was the last place in Britain where rum was to be had. My taste had changed several times since she fixed her notion of what I liked: but I'd never been able to bring myself to undermine any of those legends of hers. The meals I ate in the bungalow were anthologies of items I'd loved, or expressed unwise pleasure in, thirty or forty years before.

So I drank my rum and we drifted into the hall, on the way out, via unlockings and unchainings, to the car. As always, my father's mood had become boisterously wistful. We'd come; he'd resisted our presence, throughout the poisoned opening phase; there'd been the joviality of lunch, and of the drive to the sea afterwards, and my father's five minutes of cautious excursion across the pebbles; then the collapse into nastiness on our return. Now he realised it was all over, and was sorry. I think all his life he'd discovered the likeability of certain occasions only when he'd made them intensely unlikeable and they were drawing to a close.

Also—Kate often made this point—he perhaps realised that we weren't what, between visits, he imagined us to be. In their absence, he re-invented people, according to his general notion of mankind as creatures compounded of treachery, guile—double-dealers, every one. He hated my amiability (I was often rueful about it myself, but that's another matter), yet towards the end of many of these visits would become

33

affected by it. Not long before, he'd protested. 'You've got a good word to say for everybody. It drives me up the wall sometimes.' And, of course, it did. It wasn't that I was spectacularly good-natured: but that any sort of mildness of opinion and anxiety to look at a question (or a person) from more than one angle made my father furious. Most of my life, dammit, I'd enraged and frustrated him by having inherited, not his angry temper, but my mother's friendly one.

He was driven by a dark nature: it grew darker with time, and dismayed even him. But an equal dismay was caused him by the mildness he'd married and engendered. It threatened the wholeness of his philosophy. Much of the time he felt bound to set about the undermining of those who offered this threat, by ascribing to them motives even more underhand than those he attributed to opponents sharing his temperament. He would amaze you with the horrid reasons he'd invent for your most innocent action. And when you were out of sight, he redesigned you, according to principles all the more hideous because, for a moment, he'd been tempted to like and enjoy you . . .

Now he made familiar jokes as he donned his sloppiest hat (it was the most formally sloppy hat I'd ever seen) to keep the fatal chills at bay when he waved us goodbye. So I made *my* familiar joke: tapping, not the barometer that hung for decorative rather than informative reasons in the hall, but the framed citation next to it which recorded my father's enrolment as a Member of the Order of the British Empire.

On a recent visit my father had broken the news to me (it was clearly how he thought of it; I was given beer to support me in my inevitable grief) that he had not willed this tedious document to me, but to my sister. 'You know who you are,' he explained, tight-lipped. 'She doesn't. She needs reminding.' My father had always held it against my brother-in-law that he'd stripped my sister of her true surname, replacing it with one that was necessarily not of the same standard. I was quite dazed for a moment, trying to imagine Betty being made adequately conscious of her maiden name by the possession of this perfunctory parchment.

Lord, I remembered when my father went to the Palace for his MBE. Afterwards, he invited us to join him at a London restaurant. When the bill came, he was totally surprised by it.

34

He had never before eaten in such a place, and had sadly under-estimated the cost of doing so. There was a moment when he found it necessary to confess as much; even more painfully, to borrow from his son and his son-in-law in order to make up the sum. I was close to tears for him; the quavering grandeur of the event was awfully undermined. But worse was to come. My father must have added a tip of the size customary in a teashop. We were on our way out, our magnificence slowly being re-established, the new MBE superb in his new black suit, holding his new black Homburg, when the waiter made his calculation and rushed after us with tempestuous exclamations of disbelief and rage. My father stared at him, unable to understand in what way he'd offended. 'The tip ... ' my brother-in-law hissed. 'He needs a bigger tip.' My father looked dazed. 'Should be ten per cent of the bill.' 'Needs more money,' my father mumbled, and felt in his pockets for what remained. And then, to the vibrating waiter, and handing over an uncounted miscellany of coins: 'I'm very sorry. I'm afraid I didn't understand your customs.'

It had a forlorn dignity, a brave absurdity, father's self-excusal: it even slightly put the waiter, the restaurant, the whole world of such restaurants, in the wrong, not only for having such practices but for failing to ensure that they were popular knowledge. If I could have arranged that my father's celebration of that mechanical honour went without a hitch, I'd have done it, and even given a particle of my soul in exchange. But reflection suggests that such smoothness was not in his line. Even at the rare moments when he felt fortunate, his life insisted on its essential jagged nature.

In any case, I suppose one must say ... what a moment of revenge for the innumerable bus conductors, cinema ushers, shop assistants and other persons he had so remorselessly reported—and taken their numbers when they had numbers —on the strength of small dissatisfactions. Servants of one kind or another to whom this civil servant, alas, had behaved most uncivilly.

... So we stood in the garden, and my father's wistful joviality was at its height. He even gestured towards his neighbour to the east, not the offender with the untrimmed laburnums, but a new man, with whom, my father was

35

indicating, something positively like friendship had been established. It was friendship, of course, very much in his own style, and he defined it in the crisp manner he employed when he feared that reckless warmth might be detected in some action of his: 'We don't go in there when we want to, and they don't come in here when they want to.' It occurred to me that my father's idea of being in Heaven would involve camping at a substantial distance outside the Pearly Gates ...

My mother liked the new neighbour, she said (she who liked most people), because, like my father, he tended his garden without help. 'He does it all off his own back.'

'I don't suppose Catherine will want to kiss me,' said my father as we made ready to go: and Kate kissed him twice and said, 'And I don't care if the neighbours do see!' He was laughing enormously about this, which in other circumstances would have been an unforgiveable remark and no joke at all, as we successfully drove between his front gates (Kate had a recurrent nightmare in which she drove at instead of through them: 'I'd go straight back to London at 100 m.p.h. if that happened,' she'd warned me) and, feeling moved in a very bruised fashion, turned towards home.

I had my usual two thoughts in mind. My mother looked like someone who, after all, hadn't been rescued. And that jovial mood wouldn't last; soon, the air would again be full of chairs and knives.

6

'So,' said one man to another, 'how was Buenos Aires?' 'Warsaw,' said the other, as though it was not much of a correction. 'Of course. . . . Good?' 'Rotten,' said the first.

I reflected how laconic the reporting of the world's affairs might be if it were recorded in the BBC lift ...

Jenny, my producer, was already in the studio. 'My God,' she said. 'Here comes that *fool!* How are you, love?'

I was a fool, according to Jenny, because I had this weakness of being instantly inclined to like people, rather than to reserve judgement pending massive inquiries into their characters. 'What a pleasant man,' I'd say, after some encounter; and Jenny would fix me with amazed eyes. 'You're absolutely right, love—except that he's a *total shit!*' I was a fool also because of the hypochondria that was the scourge of my middle years, worse than any actual illness. It was to take me a decade of twinges, prowling aches, numbnesses and digestive mysteries to realise that the human system is subject to constant alarms of the sort, and that, on the basis of my own experience, these rarely led to death. By the time I was fifty I'd begun to weary of taking fright. I had worn through such delusions as that a tongue ought to have a smooth surface (oh the agony when I noticed for the first time that the surface was fissured, and supposed this to be a fresh and fatal defect of my own tongue), and that if it hurt when you pressed down on it fiercely with a finger it was not because there was some malign growth inside it, but because you had pressed down on it fiercely with a finger. Jenny had grown accustomed to discovering that under my general cheerfulness I was usually worrying about some unmistakeable pointer to early extinction.

There was an occasion when I was recording a discussion with a young and promising Ugandan short story writer who had a subtle way, I thought, with dialogue. He did not oblige his characters to make unlikely speeches. Indeed, he could so place the clichés of everyday conversation that they told their own story, often by their attempt not to tell it. 'Well,' said Sam, replying to my praise, 'if I said to you conversationally, "How are you?", you would give an equally brief and conventional reply, wouldn't you? You wouldn't make a long speech of it!' The recording came to a halt while Jenny rolled about behind the glass. 'You *fool!*' she said affectionately to Sam. I realised that there were now at least two of us. A comforting hundred per cent increase in fools.

There was another young producer in the studio this morning who was going to read extracts from the poems I was discussing. We'd once had African readers: but if they came from West Africa, there were complaints of unintelligibility from East Africa: and the other way round. So now, most of the time, we stuck to English voices.

They weren't easy poems for anyone to read, these. They were by a young Ghanaian whose natural tone, I'd sometimes thought, was the shout. He was a prodigious bellower. No subject he broached was so much discussed as invoked. It was O everything. O Africa! O love! and O me! because the poet was enormously impressed by himself, and was given to converting his curriculum vitae (which included attendance at universities in Britain, Sweden and America) into pages full of exclamation marks. O Leeds! O Stockholm! O Chicago! I'd chaired a reading of his in London, on his last visit. He'd interspersed his vibrant recitations with exegesis that was just as vibrant, as full of the vocative. At one point he read lines from other African poets, in a suddenly small withered voice, crying at intervals: 'Feebleness!' or 'Lack of talent!' Then he went back to reading his own work. 'That is Genius!' he cried, the capital letter audible. And I shrank within myself, and then thought what an ass I was to do so. Because the poet's enormous self-esteem was probably not in the least like English smugness. It was a gaudy habit for which, I was fairly sure, I had no suitable words. He came from a world large and open, not to be described in the vocabulary of a northerner whose world was carefully enclosed and measured. Well, I could see already, before going to Africa, that it might be the difference between what was made of you by great constancies of weather, total sunshine followed by periods of total rain, and what was made of you by the hourly uncertainties of a northern climate.

Oh, I had no doubt that the poet was, on the whole, noisily empty. But if I spoke of his brashness I was probably using a northern word of little relevance. Years of my paper Africa had convinced me that there was much here for which I had no relevant words at all ...

Meanwhile, I was saying what I could. These were short poems, rather—as if Tintoretto had turned his hand to miniatures. 'I think as I've always felt about his verse, that it contains really rather more vague splendour of sound, rather more splutter and spit, rather more vulnerable imagery than poetry should contain. On the other hand, it does have great whole-heartedness, conviction, energy, force—whatever it is, it's not milk-and-water verse.'

And that was true. It was what I'd felt in the poet's physical presence. By all sorts of standards, he was a noisy ass—but such a vivid, live ass. A tall, beautiful shouter! But when I talked of shouting, I was perhaps being European again.

Jenny said, 'I've been in touch with Voice of Kenya and Radio Uganda ... I think they know what they're doing. They'll have plans for you when you arrive.'

She looked like someone who thought they wouldn't know what they were doing, at all. It was part of that general doubt as to whether, for example, any African booked to appear on the programme would actually arrive, at a precise hour on a precise day in, precisely, Bush House. (Some, it was said, were suddenly struck by the name of the building, and stayed angrily away.) The African sense of time. But that was part of this Africanness of which I was aware, the antithesis of Englishness. We were all White Rabbits in the cool north, watches in hand, hurrying about to keep warm. If warmth had been guaranteed all over the earth, would the idea of punctuality ever have arisen?

Jenny came from a family, French by connection and character, who'd resigned themselves to the English pronunciation of their name: which was Mallet. She was in many respects thoroughly London suburban; but her local qualities were frayed and foreign at the edges. Round the rim of herself she was vaguely but strongly un-English: there was some sense of her being at home anywhere abroad as she never was ... at home. Her existence had mysterious extensions in Greece and America. Indeed, there were rumours of ... Kurds in her background—or was it Pathans? People, I thought, given to riding small hairy horses. Returned from holiday, she glowed darkly as no precise northern European would have done.

She had adopted my family, all my affairs, and seemed to me, from time to time, far more attentive to them than I was myself. She had that sort of ... sympathetic habit of mind. Sometimes I thought it was connected to the gifts that made her so good a radio producer. She was accustomed to gathering all the fragments of a topic and transferring them

39

without loss to the space provided by fifteen minutes or a half hour. So now, having said all there was to say about my coming visit to East Africa, she inquired after Kate's mother.

7

Kate's mother, Dorothy, was mildly unwell, in that house of hers and Jim's that I so disliked. It had thin doors. I was depressed by the curiously frail sound they made when you closed them. There was a front room, occupied by an unplayable piano; a painting that appeared to record the moment when a flat expanse of meadow was smeared with pink blancmange; the ruin of a radiogram that Jim was always about to convert into something splendid; and many cactuses. These unpleasing plants were Dorothy's special love, and for some reason she leaned towards the worst examples. In particular she liked those that resembled the shrunken heads of old women, topped with sparse and straggling white hair. These dreadful decapitations lined the window-sill; they were the first things you saw as you approached the front door. The worst of it was that Dorothy's own hair was white and thin in that fashion: so it sometimes looked as though, as the fruit of some fearful experiment, a dozen shrunken versions of her were sitting with their backs to the window.

Such an experiment would have been Jim's, I guess. He was an engineer, a machine toolmaker; as much by instinct and knack, I think, as by training or study. He was always, with enormous hands, at work on something immensely delicate—often tentative, a little adventure in assembling parts that were of near-invisible exactitude. His hands, as well as being the biggest I'd ever seen, were twisted and incomplete. He'd lost fingers in a lathe; and both hands had been ... screwed round out of the true, seemed to be the effect ... in a road accident. Coming home tired one night, he'd driven his Austin Seven actually under the tail of a lorry, where it had been crushed, and parts of Jim with it.

He spent much of his home life in a shed in the garden, where his lathe was, and shelves full of unfinished little marvels of precise engineering. He was a profoundly unambitious man with a gift that he sold to his employers for a ridiculously low wage, and offered freely to any friend who wanted something made that was difficult enough to be of delight to Jim. Wherever he'd lived during his married life there'd been a shed or similar refuge; he and Dorothy had little in common, and he hated the company of her cactuses. He was boyish, severely shy, from a family that had been brought up by a shy, stern father. Kate remembered that she'd pray for him not to take her for a walk when she was little. He clearly felt it was his duty to do so, from time to time, but had nothing whatever to say to a daughter. It was agony by way of his shy, bothered silence, she said, and the grunts and odd whistlings with which he tried to make it less apparent to his small distressed companion.

When I'd gone to ask for Kate's hand—'And the rest of me,' Kate urged, and we thought of making a shameless inventory and reading it out to Jim, but decided he might not be amused—he'd hidden in the lavatory, knowing what I was there for; and I'd almost concluded that I must look elsewhere for a wife when he entered and exclaimed: 'Well, we've brought her up to be independent.' I wasn't sure if the remark was intended to make me feel I'd chosen well, or badly. With a mother who frowned on adventurousness of any kind, Kate had in fact set out to be moderately unmanageable. Jim might have been referring to this.

Unable for any reason to reach his shed, he always escaped to the lavatory. I wondered how he could endure the pokerwork admonition that hung there—Dorothy's choice —and that almost reconciled me to humourlessness. 'The day on which you have not laughed,' it said, 'is a day lost.' The house was a suffocating nest of rooms, and entering it nowadays made me behave badly; largely, I guess, because it resembled the house in which I'd been smothered as a boy and youth. I wanted to make terrible, rude jokes, to clown and sing. I'd compromise by taking Dorothy's hat from where it hung in the hall; a sort of large tea-cosy in appearance, with rudimentary wings. I'd put it on my head and enter the room wearing it; Dorothy would laugh uncertainly.

It was a semi-detached house round the corner from the similar semi-detached house and stifling nest of rooms in which I'd spent over twenty years of my life. Jim and Dorothy rented theirs from the council: the house I'd lived in till my marriage had cost my father £800, paid in instalments weekly, with interest, to a dapper little man, Mr Bloomfield; as a child I'd watched him admiringly as he made copper-plate entries in the book in which was recorded the slow dissolution of the debt. He was enormously polite; no collector of moneys could have done more to charm the painful element out of his visits. I took him to be a rather eccentric kind of family friend.

Now all these 1920-ish houses were trying hard to belong to the 1960s. The windows that were natural to them, with their small panes, had been ripped out and replaced by picture windows. From outside the picture was of small rooms crammed with furniture; from within the picture was of the house opposite, its natural windows ripped out and replaced by picture windows. Still standing in the road where we'd lived was the first garage the road had ever boasted, a cause of annoyance to my father, who saw it as an intolerable claim to superiority. ('They needn't think I'm impressed.') Now every house had its car, or cars, but few had been able to make room for garages. So there were cars at the kerbside, unbroken uneasinesses of metal from top to bottom of the road. There were front gardens that had been uprooted and replaced with cement, with cars standing on them, staring into the nearest picture windows.

I couldn't bear to look at No. 10. My father's privet hedges, which he'd kept marvellously shaven for thirty years, had gone, together with the rosebeds and the bird bath in cement that I'd designed, and my father had executed: unpleasing but unpretentious. It was my first, and last, bird bath. On the pink surface that had replaced all these stood two small cars. The front window, which had been a mystery of net curtains, with my mother as often as not sitting behind them, keeping a gossip's watch on her neighbours, had been removed in favour of a single sheet of glass, revealing everything. My father would have been appalled, even now that he was a

42

hundred miles away, to know that a room once his could be raked by the insolent eyes of any passer-by.

Relations between our sets of parents had never been good. My father's rejection of the Browns began, I suppose, with his rejection of Kate.

It is scarcely possible to imagine anyone married to a child of his who wouldn't have qualified, by the very fact of that marriage, for his hostility. It was, in his view, a classic case of a stranger using a sly device (in this case, marriage) to bring about intimate contact with him. Detecting in Kate certain firmnesses of character, this most tyrannical of men decided that she had married me in order to have a foolish slave ever at hand. 'We think,' he said once, 'that when you are on the downstairs phone to us, Catherine is on the upstairs phone, making sure you say the right thing.' It's an example of how he re-invented us once we were out of sight. Faced with this hideous fantasy, I turned pale, was ready to storm—but he raised his terrible hand. 'No point in getting worked up,' he declared. 'We think what we think.'

He thought what he thought about Kate's parents, too. They were worse than Kate herself, claiming acquaintance from a position of at least one remove. If this sort of thing went on, one would find oneself exposed, on slender grounds of kinship, to any Tom, Dick or Harry whatever. (And countless prattling Harriets.)

To my father, Kate's father was, invariably, 'Brown.' He was, as it happened, as unlikely as anyone to win my father's approval. He'd fought in his county's yeomanry in the First World War: my father had fought in a regiment thoroughly Cockney. Jim was deeply shy, rural in background; my father had no shyness at all, and was profoundly urban. Jim was a peasant, a saddler's son: a man whose hands (maimed and twisted as they were) mattered. My father was essentially compounded of London's grit. His hands (though so green in private) had a fundamental commitment to official ink.

Then my father was obsessively neat in appearance. I'd known him destroy a snapshot because it showed a turn-up on his trousers accidentally turned *down*. Jim on the other hand wore shapeless clothes of carefully maintained shabbiness. Whenever Kate, when she was living at home, bought something new he'd say, '*Now* we shall be burgled!' Being

43

shabby was a message to all thieves: Try somewhere else—there's nothing here!

The difference between the two men constituted, at the same time, a dangerous similarity. Jim had a rural independence to which my father responded with the urban equivalent—in his case, of course, carried to monstrous extremes. There had been an early encounter between the two that set the pattern. Soon after our marriage my parents—he in his most inhuman bowler hat, she in some terrifying female equivalent—made their way down the few minutes of roadway that separated their home from that of Kate's parents. I think Jim and Dorothy already knew what to expect: there had been indicative little coolnesses at the wedding. But they must have been (who ever escaped being?) surprised by the full character of my father's unwillingness to fraternise. The meeting would have gone badly even if it had not started badly; as it did by reason of Jim's shy failure to be present. He was, Dorothy explained, in the workshop, finishing something delicate and urgent. ('My train,' Kate hazarded, on hearing the story. Nearly thirty years before, when Jim perhaps cherished hopes that the mistake in his only child's sex might be reversed, he'd begun to create for her this stunningly exact model of one of the great locomotives of the 1920s. It was, like so much else in Jim's life, perpetually prevented from completion.) My father must have sat fuming: half-ready to replace the bowler hat on his head and leave. When Jim at last appeared, feigning amazement at the passage of time, there were barked exchanges. My father went in, on these occasions, for a nasty kind of laughter, cut very short indeed. The women engaged in a sighing detente, on the edge of the central encounter: Jim laughing unpleasantly in his own way—which involved a kind of insulting conspiracy between himself and his moustache. He must have indulged his habit, brought on by any social occasion, of beating his knees with his huge injured hands: which would have brought my father close to crying, 'Oh, for God's sake don't *fidget!*' It's what he'd shouted at me thousands of times for much slighter symptoms of restlessness.

At the end, which was not long in coming, my father rose and said (I guess, with as little sincerity as he could manage) that the Browns must return the visit. 'Thank you,' said Jim,

44

with, I think, *total* sincerity. 'But we are too attached to our own home for much visiting.' My father, looking for any bludgeon to beat Kate with, would years later refer to the final moment of this social event; when he and my mother stepped through the Browns' front door and, in Jim's hands, it at once slammed to behind them.

Never, in the sullen history of relations between our sets of parents, would there be any equivalent of standing at an open door, smilingly bidding farewell to the parting guests. Their every meeting thereafter had the character of doors being sensationally slammed.

8

To keep afloat as a freelance, it was necessary to take on too much (for fear that tomorrow would offer too little), yet never to fail to deliver on time. I had two very strong feelings about the life this led to: one of simple delight, and one of simple horror. Most of the time they were mixed up; I was delightedly horrified.

Going to Africa—well, going anywhere—for four weeks was like sitting down to stare at the view whilst being pursued by a howling mob. Some things had to be done at twice the usual speed: some twice as often as usual (so with my BBC programmes, being stockpiled against my absence). Some items had to be pushed ahead of me, under the carpet of the future. It was a transparent carpet, alas, and they'd be there, awfully visible, when I returned.

Enterprises that simply could not be interrupted had to be persuaded of the possibility of interruption. Among these was the putting together of an encyclopaedia of education that I'd been fool enough (in Jenny's sense, but also in my own) to agree to edit. My aim that it should be entirely free of professional jargon had turned out to be at odds with the aim of my two hundred or so contributors, who had resolved that

professional jargon should be what it was exclusively composed of. I was rewriting nearly everything. Topics on which
I'd invited articles of 100 words were dealt with in 1000
words: the accompanying note always said, 'It is rather longer
than you asked for; but please feel free to cut.' This ignored
the fact that anything written in 1000 words has a style and
spread that do not lend themselves to surgical reduction by
nine-tenths. I felt savagely free to cut, but was more often
fumingly obliged to remould. The chief agony was that many
of the contributors had an elastic sense of time. I had to write
letters of editorial surprise followed by letters of editorial
amazement. I found myself wishing that the whole affair had
been like an examination, my contributors present and visible
in their desks, I pacing up and down as invigilator.

On top of this, there were persons of some academic
distinction whom I longed simply to thrash.

I fitted in lectures: an activity that always astonished me.
How did it come about that I spent so much of my time
telling stories to teachers and others, which is what it usually
amounted to, because I could make my way towards general
conclusions only by reflecting on particular cases? As
someone absolutely not given to attending lectures, I was
puzzled by my audiences and their amiable appetite. A few
days before I was to fly away, I went to a northern city to
speak to a women's luncheon group. They'd asked me to talk
about Education Today, and I'd imagined that the sober
choice of title indicated a sober concern on their part. I was
quite wrong about this. I knew it the moment I took my seat
among these ladies, with their chattering hats. The chairman's introduction had largely related to flower arrangement.
She was intense about flower arrangement, and what she said
was followed intensely by her listeners, who hissed and
tittered and sighed as if some appalling scandal were being
reported. Perhaps it was. She came to me gloomily. I think
she'd already decided that I was not their sort of person. 'Mr
Bilshen,' she said, with a firmness that made me uncertain of
the case for believing that this was not my name. I rose,
defeated before I began by a sensation of being unpopular in
unfamiliar circumstances. I felt, in floral terms, horribly
ill-arranged.

The railway station: three days to go, a hundred things to

do, and here, after ruining the midday meal of a large group of women, I was in the urinal—sighing loudly, I was surprised to notice—and dwarfed. The station was in the grandest Victorian manner, and this urinal was designed for piddlers twenty feet tall ...

I'd also been to look at a famous unorthodox school, of which I'd been asked to write a profile. I spent two pleasant days coming to agreeable conclusions about it; and on the last night was invited to a secret confabulation in a dormitory, where a group of children assured me that the original ideals of the place were being subtly (and, of course, charmingly) abandoned. The school had been in a rut, but now it was getting out of the rut on the wrong side. I withdrew with two plausible pictures of the place, quite different from each other. 'Look here upon this picture and on this ...' I pushed it under the carpet.

Back at home I settled down to bring my diary up-to-date. My son Tom dictated a possible entry: 'Going to visit that school was pleasant. It was a shock to come back to Tom and Dan.'

Tom, I was aware, was watching me sharply, ruthlessly; I felt helplessly unsatisfactory, as my father had appeared to me when I was Tom's age. That was when I'd so powerfully taken against the poor man's walking with hands clasped on his stomach. I thought how the biological odds are heaped up against human beings. It is necessary for a child's security that its parents should seem perfect, unimproveable ... until the child reaches the age of, say, ten. Then comes the discovery that grown-ups are not remotely perfect—indeed, that they are flawed beyond belief. From being the fount of truth they become the fount of all falsehood. In the first rage of this perception your child turns a disenchanted eye on the nearest adults: his parents. They are usually at that moment entering middle age, and are curiously in need of being bolstered rather than debunked. They have never been more reluctant to stand in as models of human rottenness.

Tom at eighteen had years of disenchantment behind him; had become a master of prickliness; brought to bear on my distracted life a severity of judgement that would have led to the impeachment of a saint. Yet he was reading E. M. Forster,

47

and kept appearing in my room with a new phrase to enthuse over ... My son, this world-weary enthusiast.

As for Dan, he had begun to do biology at school, and was overwhelmed by a rush of brand-new knowledge: science in the guise, largely, of the improbable. Unable to prevent himself from lecturing us about it, he was embarrassed and did so in an assumed voice.

And the last programmes.

My paper Africa was a flesh-and-blood Africa, too. There'd been, quite early—before the programme became weekly instead of monthly—visits to Leeds, where several writers were doing post-graduate work; or, in the case of the most gifted one of them, post-graduate novel-writing. With *him*, this man who couldn't help being a novelist, one night in a room that looked as though it had been bombed by books, defending against the rest the probably indefensible view that no great work of literature had ever emerged from an evil mind. It was before mission-given first names were abandoned: he was still James. There was Desiderio, the severest linguist; and Albert, who was to become one of the first home-grown critics of African writing; and Timothy, who wrote small nervous poems. They were East Africans: their work, I thought, that of writers anxious to say not a word more than was strictly accurate and fitting for the occasion that caused them to write. I used to suggest, in those days, that the great East African novel would turn out to be—given some relaxation of the original posture—eight hundred words long. How different from the ebullient West, tending to ... ebullience. I'd be publicly very certain about this sort of thing; within myself, would falter, doubt if such generalisations could ever be valid. Yet—look again, and wasn't the East (in terms of flesh-and-blood as well as paper) so austere, so classical, and the West so extravagant, so romantic?

And there was my friend Biddy, from Sierra Leone, who'd written stories about diamond smugglers; and now didn't write at all, being busy converting himself into a civil engineer. Well, for many it was an activity with no deep roots, or they had other engrossing work to do, in a continent where there were no full-time writers. Such a muddle of the giftless, the deeply amateur, the confusingly talented, and

48

those whose gifts were wonderfully evident, and capably employed. The usual elements of the literary scene: but an unusual scene. Well, for one thing there was that general reaching for the pen, partly because you might, when whole areas of the past were being wiped out within a fraction of a lifetime, be able to preserve something: childhood of a kind never to be repeated, an old man's story that would never be told again.

The birth of a new literature under the world's largely indifferent nose! With, already, such contrasts! In Nigeria, Chinua Achebe's examination, in skilful quiet English, of the gulf between the new and the old, between what the white man had brought, good and bad, and the black man had always had: good and bad. And Cyprian Ekwensi, first of Nigeria's novelists to be made much of—largely, I guess, because Nigeria had need of a novelist, along with the other accoutrements of independence. Ekwensi wrote novels that were violent, hectic, brimming with the excitement of Nigerian urban life; they drew very largely on the sometimes absurd vocabulary and phrasing of the novelette. I remembered—flesh-and-blood!—Ekwensi telling me how he always had in mind his fellow Africans sitting in buses and, out of their enormous appetite for words, making themselves read the dull pages of newspapers. He'd thought at one time of walking round the country with his novels on his back, selling them as he went. One early problem: how did you feed a largely unfed popular audience?

And another problem: how, in the early days of a literature, when everything was acclaimed with a shout, did you introduce notions of discrimination? 'You write one novel,' said Achebe, 'and you become a spokesman.'

Here was a literature, still largely published in London, which had to be international before it was local. How was such an oddity to be judged—given that a literature ought to emerge from its own immediate world; a little of it by remorseless sifting being found of interest to the world beyond?

And what of the fact that English was for none of these a first tongue?

'Nira', said one of the stories in those last programmes before my trip, 'soon found herself in Oyoyo's tender arms. A

49

true romantic picture dawned on them.' Later, Oyoyo's chest was 'rising and falling like the graceful galloping of a limousine.' Oyoyo was embarrassed: would she not notice how he stared at her juicy limbs? He found an answer to his problem: 'As a pastime, he was looking with anxiety at his double scotch.'

Sometimes such phrases sprang from a simple misunderstanding of what could be done with English. But behind them often, I'd guess, must lie the quality and spirit of some African tongue, attempting to have its way with this marvellously compliant language.

My father wrote: 'We hope Ted will look after himself in Africa. We think he gets too excited about these African writers, and ought to take it easy. He has always tended to suffer from a weak chest. He will have to do a lot of travelling. We have always found that a sense of humour helps, and not taking things too seriously. Ted has never known when to relax.' And so on.

My father's use of the word 'we', as my mother was always whisperingly confirming, was quite unauthorised. 'You and I are alike,' she'd said, recently: and then, looking across at the crouching armchair, which happened to be empty, 'I'll get a black eye in a minute!'

Kate's mother, poorly among her cactuses, said she hoped I wouldn't find her very much worse on my return. Kate's father smiled healthily and said he hoped it wouldn't be too like Egypt, where he'd been in the Great War. From his recollections, there was an ominous preponderance of sand, and a vast likelihood of sunstroke.

Kate said: 'Enjoy Africa.'

PART TWO

1

From this fatly hissing tube, a first view of the continent as we fell slowly towards Nairobi. Nothing, to begin with, but the most naked rock. Not, in that immense space, one green thing, or a flicker of movement. Then, as this invader from London twisted down over bare hills, the first scratches of husbandry, a few square shapes that were huts. Now there was a river below us. We turned and turned and the huge sun caught one bend of water and another; there were explosions of light each of which for a split second destroyed the entire scene, consumed it with bursting fire. And so we came down to a flashing of grounded metal. I stepped out only to recoil: it was as if I'd walked into a fine day in the highest possible English summer, closely wrapped in several electric blankets.

Walter Ellis met me, busily, as if I'd been some mildly inconvenient parcel. Hmm, he said ... welcome. He'd leave me at the Norfolk Hotel to rest from the journey—then perhaps I'd cross the road to the British Council office and my timetable could be discussed. I felt he meant that he would then undo the string and see what was inside the parcel, in respect of its capacity to be timetabled. It was a schoolmasterly term; later I discovered that a schoolmaster was what, for many years, Walter Ellis had been.

We were driving into the city between astonishing banks of bougainvillaea: white, purple, pink. I murmured my bewitchment. Ah, said Walter, yes. They were splendid ... He hoped we could draw up a timetable enjoyable to me and useful to them ...

And then I was lying on my bed in a wing of the Norfolk, while from everywhere about me came the sound of non-stop excitement—particularly of laughter: the shouted delight of men and women, the deep chortle of parrots, the chittering of

53

other birds. Well, clearly I'd always misused the phrase 'the open air.' Before this I'd had no notion of its meaning. Outside, beyond the walls and windows of my little room— which were hardly able to create a sense of insideness—the air was fantastically open. It was also full of staggering sunshine, and, from time to time, of what I was to discover was a perfect proof of your being in Africa: the sound of innumerable things being very loudly wound up.

Lying dazed under the beautiful knot of my mosquito net, all clothes flung off, I felt that behind this experience of my arrival in Africa, so burningly close to the Equator, lay another, remote, unlikely—but somehow the perfect preparation for this one. And then it dawned on me—it was, of course, *Alice in Wonderland*, first read in an English bed on gentle summer evenings nearly forty years before. DRINK ME, it said on the bottle, and Alice drank it and became tiny or enormous, or experienced some dramatic shift of scene. So it was now with travel. You boarded a plane and the consequences were as drastic as those produced by any draught from a bottle. Suddenly the sun was twice the size it had been before: the air was filled with flying bananas and winged pillar boxes: the people were gleamingly and happily black. Every corner of the scene was stuffed with colour, bold, elementary.

And it all (recedingly as I fell asleep) shouted, gulped, gobbled, sang, spat and enormously laughed.

2

The official opening of Book Week (which would actually be a fortnight). The hall was decked with brightly painted shields and animal heads; it looked as though it might belong to some Victorian sportsman whose walls had been under attack by unVictorian paintpots. Lower down, but not very much lower down, were the books, mounted on pegboards, themselves standing on high easels. Only Kenyans of an average height of ten feet could have handled those books, I reflected, as distinct from peering at them uncertainly from below.

I met the distinguished older novelist with whom, absurdly, I was representing British letters. I had admired him since adolescence, and something young and severe inside me looked on disapprovingly while I addressed him with scandalous friendliness. We drank sherry, very sharp, so that I had an instant stomach-ache. I was then driven by someone from the British Council to his home in a dusky suburb. Like the sherry, the house was not particularly African: it had a sprawling Spanish quality, and stood among large lawns that might have been English, except that they were brown rather than green and that un-English insects were soliloquising with high-pitched coarseness in the grass. He went away on some educational errand, leaving me to his wife, who said, 'It's *very* English here!' I wondered, with dismay, if she was trying to make me at home when I so much wanted to be abroad. She led me into the house, which was in darkness. I was ready, of course, for any astonishment, but all the same was startled when she called out at once, in tones of hectoring panic, 'Philip! Rebecca!' To the shadowy figure that appeared, she cried, 'The lights! The lights!' I assumed that something had happened to the electricity that perhaps was threatening all our lives—even, given the angry shrillness of her cries, the entire city. But it appeared that she wanted the lights to be turned on. Rebecca, an unhappy-looking woman, touched the switches, and there was light. The switches were a foot from where we were standing.

Brilliant children she happened to have, she said. But of course, so difficult to find the right schooling for them here. So many European teachers were leaving because of the Government's policy of Africanisation. Well, little Keith was her eldest. She *must* tell me this and that and another story illustrative of his quickness of mind. Here, of course, it was threatened ...

It seemed curiously horrible to be spending my first evening in Africa and to be listening to dissatisfactions common in the suburbs of London. It was like coming to

Africa and yet, in some banal fashion, not coming to it at all.

But I came to it, very early the next morning.

My friend Colin was teaching in the University College of Nairobi. He'd said I must at the first opportunity come and see the animals in the National Park, preferably at dawn. Well, next morning, eh? He'd call at ... 5.30. I put it to the receptionist at the Norfolk that I should be called at 5.20. 'Make it five-fifteen, will you?' she said. 'If an African's on duty, he can understand five o'clock or five-fifteen, but an odd time like five-twenty will confuse him, and he will ignore it altogether.'

My newcomer's hair stood on end. Wasn't such a remark based on some notion of African ... oh, innumerateness couldn't be the word? Incapacity simply to master the clock ...? Then I looked at her pleasant sensible face, and remembered those occasions back at the BBC when the studio manager had been obliged to record: DNM. Did Not Materialise. A contributor had been thrown, not just by a fine matter of five minutes, but by the precise naming of a day. I made it 5.15.

A difference between being northern and being equatorial. That's what it was. I must watch this. It was clearer than ever that the clouds told one story, the sun another.

And so, just before dawn, we arrived at the gates of the National Park, embellished with metal lions. And in a moment were inside, and the Park was endless around us. Curious experience: going through a gate into the unenclosed. I thought of the local park at home, the Rec, and the old parkie, Flannelbum, who'd spent much of his working life at war with the local kids. The first time I'd heard a grown-up use the word 'sod'—when old Flannelbum was driving a jeering gang of us towards the lower gates, c. 1929: 'Get out, you little sods, and stay out.' Strangely, my father and my uncles had not been given to the word. I'd thought till then that it was reserved for juvenile use. Now, as we drove towards the sudden African brightness, I thought of Flannelbum and wondered how he'd have made out as parkie in a place as vast as this—and as fierce.

It was the Garden of Eden, surely. (Flannelbum on duty *there*! Well, God had had it easier with Adam and Eve, in

56

matters of expulsion, than Flannelbum with us.) The sun rose as if someone were punching a balloon up from the horizon, but before its appearance there was a vast flush of light, a paradoxically strong pallor followed by a deepening pink and then by the sheer flame of day. The thorn trees stood against all that light, black tangles, and on every spiky branch were revealed maribous, those black-gowned birds, standing, like speechless judges, hands behind backs, brooding on verdicts and sentences.

Everything was endless. Someone had thought it made sense, in such space, to erect signposts promising rhino, zebra, giraffe. ('To the tennis courts,' it said in the Rec at home.) I felt with relief that these domesticating touches didn't work at all. It *was* Eden. There was Colin's Peugeot blundering across it, and soon there'd be other motorised voyeurs: but the fact of Eden remained, unaffected. Here, suddenly, were nervous troops of Thomson's gazelles. They were browsingly alert, combining an effect of considerable serenity with instant readiness to bolt. Their tails revolved, revolved. I imagined a young one complaining: Oh mum, my tail's stopped. Now there were impala: they'd been to the barber's and asked for short back and bottom. We came to a slick, crowded with mixed gazelles and gnus. Across the scene, busy on some banal police duty, trotted Detective-Sergeant Wart-hog, hasty-legged. In the middle view, a jackal engaged on his own shifty errands—carefully avoiding the worthy officer. Oh, hartebeeste and wildebeeste: caracou, eland, baboon. Now, their white the benchmark of all whiteness, their black the benchmark of all blackness, zebra—fingerprints on legs. Everywhere the odours of Eden, and the spectacle of animals moving about their business. I hadn't expected such an impression of purposeful industry. The wheels of animality revolved, there was a vast deal of clocking in; clearly, everywhere there were foremen. The long redness above hills became the glare of day. We came upon my favourites: tall as exclamation marks, giraffe devoured, delicately, whole trees. From breakfast to breakfast they moved on their drawing-room legs. The opposite of a bull in a china shop—a giraffe in a china shop ... And here, offered as the *bonne bouche* of such a visit, were lions breakfasting on a zebra. Added to those other benchmarks, blood was a benchmark of redness. The lions were sandy vibrancies among sandy-coloured grasses. 'You see!' said Colin, who believed intellectually that Africa was something else, but came again and again to the National Park.

'There are British people here, you know,' he said, driving me back into the city, 'who sit around and complain. Can you imagine it—they live in Paradise and they complain! They don't know how to live! If I were the President, I'd throw them out ...'

In the stunning midday sun, I joined Walter Ellis. He was an odd man to be in Africa with. Kindly, stuffy, fussy. Time mattered to him desperately: make a date with *him* for 5.20 and three quarters of a second, and he'd be there at precisely that time, and grateful for an appointment decently defined for once. He was pleased with the engagements I'd committed myself to. They'd begin in earnest, in a manner capable of being satisfactorily logged, after the weekend. Meanwhile, let's go out to his house for lunch—and then into the hills?

It was another large house, in a sprawl of burnt garden. The rain was long overdue. For the first time in my life I sat under avocados, rather than expensively ate them. Walter talked, like that woman the night before, about the leaking away of European teachers. Well, the Ministry of Education made unreasonable demands, and didn't consult before it made them. You couldn't blame the teachers for not wanting to stay. It was the same in everything: make a scheme, and it would be abandoned because it was the work of a European. Awful difficulties, as between Europeans and Africans. Shyness and stiffness on the part of the latter. Well, every Saturday evening Walter took three African lads to an open-air cinema: they'd be embarrassed, going to an ordinary cinema and sitting with Europeans. They could sit with Walter in his car and relax.

Yes, I was already aware of this shyness and stiffness. Europeans seemed glib, by comparison, with their quick and ready patter. But of course, out of such company, Africans had their own quickness and readiness: the city beautifully vibrated with it. They *weren't* shy, they *weren't* stiff. All that arose out of discomforts of association. A gulf, as severe as between ... inhabitants of the Earth and Martians. I'd felt the unease of sitting in an official car with a driver who rarely spoke, and never of his own volition. Unnatural. I didn't know how you came to accept the unnatural.

Walter drove me, past tin-roofed huts and shacks, towards the Ngong hills. There was a long view of the Rift Valley, that enormous dent in the Earth's surface: as if the Earth had been dealt a karate chop. Tiny lakes, tiny forests, lay far below. We ran up into the hills, and Masai shepherd boys came out of the scrub on all sides, hands extended—for handshakes, but mostly for shillings, in return for agreeing to be photographed. Scarred legs; dusty feet; and this brisk acceptance of the value of such things, in photographic terms.

And a store, a sideways-leaning shack, strong-smelling, where Masai things were for sale: the bells they attached to their legs, to attract the lion; tobacco boxes, necklets of coloured beads. We stood in the windowless place, on the edge of that ancient global dent, and Walter Ellis was like a very experienced old teacher in an unusual school who'd come to some hideyhole of the Lower Fourth's, and was bluffly at home there, but in some fashion that made the actual inmates, complicatedly disorientated already for quite other reasons, confusingly ... not at home at all ... Walter clearly took it for granted that the old man in charge of the store understood him perfectly, and knew himself to be perfectly understood; but I had a strange feeling of the gap there might be between real understanding, and a school-masterly simplification of it.

3

I didn't like being at the Norfolk. It had a sealed-in Englishness. I felt unconvincing as a resident. Couldn't give orders in the right tone. Simply wasn't red-necked. Wasn't wearing shorts: so wasn't red-kneed, either. Wasn't accompanied by a thin-voiced wife. Was made uneasy by the expressionless faces of the far too many waiters, bellboys, porters.

It was Saturday night, and I walked myself weary round the town: my eyes still dazzled by colour. Oh, I'd never seen an African in my life before—not in his own world, clad in those fierce yellows and blues and reds. I found myself re-examining words like 'gaudy'. Gaudy, garish, lurid. Phrases like 'show off'; verbs like 'flaunt', 'prance', 'strut'. It was what I'd felt when responding back in London to that Ghanaian poet: the vocabulary of English as used by the English is marked by the prejudices of soft-hued people living in a soft-hued world. It was silly to be an African in Africa and not to be gaudy: not to flaunt, prance, strut.

And then, requiring yet another set of verbal adjustments, the Asian quarter: little girls like butterflies in their Saturday saris; little boys like oriental Etonians; and the rows of stores, oblong caverns lined on each side with bales of brilliant, but Indian, colour.

And so under my mosquito net; and then out again for the Sunday morning scene. Longing to exclaim, 'What a glorious day!' and frustrated because it simply wouldn't make sense. As I stepped out into the noisy oven of the morning, an American voice behind me cried, 'Will you smell that clear, unpolluted air!'

Half a dozen little cigarette-smoking boys, African Artful Dodgers, toughly ragged, roasting corn on a portable brazier on the busy pavement. Clearly in some way an illegal activity, because when a policeman appeared, they ran into an alleyway and vanished. Or rather, I knew only that they'd vanished, and assumed they'd run into the alleyway. They'd gone, like ragged little puffs of smoke. The policeman stared at some length at the brazier, which volunteered no information, and then passed on. Whereupon the little boys reversed the mysterious process of their disappearance, making it a mysterious process of appearance, and their leader, thin legs aggressively astride, blew in the direction of the retreating policeman the most insolent smoke-ring I'd ever seen.

And here was a Salvation Army meeting, of all things, a great ring of white-clad salvationists—and scores of children sitting in a fidgety heap at the centre of that clapping, drumming, tambourining circle. And now, a jauntily running group with banners, singing jazzily: dressed in white, too, moved by their faith, whatever it was, to great grins. They were suddenly there, and suddenly gone, a snake of song in the writhing crowd.

And so to an appointment, on the Norfolk terrace, with one of the organisers of Book Week. A piece by Peter Ngali had appeared that morning in the *Sunday Nation*, arguing for publishing African books at home in Africa, and for a cool look at the imperialism of foreign publishers. All that depended, he reasoned, on the willingness of the writer positively to seek publication on the spot. Only if he did that would local publishers be strengthened. He was calling the writers home, from London largely.

The Kenyan establishment, he said now over our beers, was Makerere-based—founded strongly on that Ugandan university. Makerere was the Oxbridge of East Africa. It had produced a ruling class that was both respectable and exclusive, and dreadfully sensitive to pressures from almost any quarter. So films were often censored at the request of embassies: leading to hilarious results, since, when this cutting was carried out, no thought was given to continuity. 'A whole Kenyan generation,' said Peter, 'is growing up believing that narrative is quite naturally something that has ridiculous gaps in it.' There was an official legend of Kenyan non-alignment. Well, films again: the only Russian film admitted to the country had been *Hamlet*.

Take, said Peter, the situation of the National Theatre —across the road there. Recent appointment of a new director, who proposed to continue with the mixture as before: that is, fifth-rate European plays performed by amateurs. At a meeting called by the new director, the man's opening statement was: 'I take it most of us here are either from England or from France.' Peter had leapt to his feet. Was there to be no *African* theatre? He'd found himself at once in the centre of a storm of ridicule. Theatre was a sophisticated art, he was told, and Africans would take a long time to adjust to it. Meanwhile ...

A fact, said Peter, that Africans were not yet playgoers. But I should look at the foyer of the National Theatre next time I was passing. The pictures that lined its walls didn't even reflect *modern* British theatre. Instead, they constituted a probably quite rare collection of photographs of Irving, Ellen Terry and so on.

I glanced across the road from time to time as Peter was talking, not at the National Theatre, but at the British Council's headquarters beyond. Kindly Walter Ellis would not approve of this sort of talk, at all. This was brittle, clever sixth-form talk, he'd judge. How could you draw stiff, shy, embarrassed Africa to ... the Old Vic, the Aldwych ... ? That's what it amounted to! It would take many reluctant, awkward years.

What did you find if you weighed Walter's consuming caution against Peter Ngali's bright probing habit of mind, and desire to bring about change?

... Kenyatta! said Peter. Senile!—he should stand down. The country's great hope lay in the University College and the people it might produce—but that was still dizzy after the upheaval of Africanisation, when Europeans were replaced, on blind principle, by Africans.

'Oh, one day,' Peter cried, 'we *will* be independent, you know. But we're a long way from it now.'

As I'd not felt at home in the Englishness of the Norfolk, so he'd been made to feel not at home in the Kenyan establishment. Well, he wore these casual coloured shirts. He'd been rebuked for it by ... an important person ... only the other day. What was the use of Peter's cleverness, his status as one of the most highly educated of young Kenyans, if these qualifications were not dressed up in a freshly laundered white shirt and silk tie?

I thought of my father. How, given any willingness to take the African scene as a real human scene, he'd have felt at home in the middle of this argument! How he'd have called Peter Ngali to order! 'I look twice at a man wearing a coloured shirt. Well, if you've nothing else to go by ...'

My father had been appalled by my mildly coloured socks. What would he make of Africa?

Given a new place, I want nothing more urgently than to go out into it and get to know it. So I went walking again that afternoon—having, as I noticed I thought of it, *slipped out* of

62

the hotel—and found myself in a strange situation. I was simply, as far as I could see, the only white person on foot in the whole city.

I walked, curiously glanced at, along the Uhuru Highway. What a road this was, in the stunning sunshine! Trees brimming with red blossom, huge succulents, little parks to this side and that, full of unfamiliar and often not strictly credible foliage. At one point I was following two women, each carrying a great burden of firewood held by a thong round the forehead. A stick dropped out of one of the bundles. I hurried forward to pick it up; the woman who'd lost it looked round at me, with a broad wicked smile, spoke what was clearly an ironical word, picked up the stick between a big toe and the next, and handed it to herself. Her smile became even more wicked.

I felt like someone who has broken the simplest rule of a simple game.

Nairobi—the real Nairobi, as I thought of it, under the Nairobi of the Norfolk and Walter Ellis and even of Peter Ngali—of all those with access to cars—the real Nairobi was singing and clapping again, at a great crossing. There were hundreds on a waste plot, who'd raised a banner that said simply 'Church'; clapping as though there might be no end to it, they cried *Hallelujah*, under umbrellas red and black. Beyond them, under a tattered awning hundreds of yards long, made out of old sacks, there was a market—a great offering of dejected objects, and infinitely worn-out clothing. And so to a shabby no-man's land where the city petered out in gloomy tenements: beginning again after a gap with raw white housing. The gap was filled with giant weeds, the hugest weeds I'd ever seen, vegetable tenements in themselves: a wide wedge of disorder, on the edge of which stood a shack of the greatest possible seediness, perhaps six or seven feet in frontage, declaring on a painted plank that it was 'Sweetheart Hotel, Associated with Supreme Hotels Ltd.'

And suddenly, I felt weary of colour, of the constant passing of vivid people with faces that promised no response to my kind of face. I was an *absolute* stranger. I might be stared at but there was no connection; I was an outsider, as I'd never been in my life before.

But, incorrigible, I walked again in the evening. It was

63

softly warm, now. Again I made my way out of the centre of the town, drawn by the fringe, the promise of ... something really Kenyan. I knew I wasn't yet in Africa. Could I ever reach it?

A boy drew up beside me: torn shirt, torn shorts. In awkward English, 'Good evening.' Could he talk to me? He was, he said, from Tanzania—was working at one of the hotels in the city; a Masai, who'd learned English for three years, had left school two years ago. At home was herdsman for the family cattle. Had three brothers and three sisters. I listened, murmured. 'I like you,' he kept saying. That was, he implied, because I would let him talk to me. 'I like you.' He tried out the English alphabet on me, walked closer, said, 'I like you more.' Yes, he did read English books. He felt in the back pocket of his shorts and brought out a travel brochure. *Germany at a Glance.* Was it a bad book? Most Europeans, he said, behaved as if they thought they were gods, and asked brusquely (he gave an imitation) what he was trying to say to them. They had no patience with his attempts to practise his English.

Did I, he asked, like womans? Yes, I said, I liked womans; so much so that I had married one. Yes, he said, but you got disease from them. Could he come and stay at my hotel that night?

When I retreated baffled from the impossibility of discussing this in the limited English at our disposal, he said he didn't know what to do. He had no money, having sent home for some and spent much of that on drink, the day being so hot. He had lodgings in Nairobi but five miles out, and he had only three shillings and the taxi would cost ten shillings ...

And I was crestfallen. I'd believed that the European who walked in Nairobi on a Sunday evening had run into the Masai who'd despaired of finding a European with whom he could practise his English, and that there'd been a pleasant breach in that wall I'd been aware of in the afternoon: between the small pampered fraction of the world, and the huge fraction of it that was savagely unpampered. And it wasn't like that at all. He was the beggar, I the begged from, according to the perfectly banal rules of the immemorial relationship between the two.

What was worse, he seemed to think that my pacing through Nairobi in search of ... good Lord ... Kenyan reality was the restiveness of someone sexually unassuaged. To walk was to be on some sort of prowl.

Oh, he must sleep out, then, I said; it was warm and wouldn't hurt. And with that I left him looking enormously sad, oh such total sadness of expression and posture, outside the hotel where he worked, or claimed to be working (already I was uncertain about everything he'd told me). But he hurried after me. I said, not having anything else to say, that it was bad to beg. 'Am I bad?' 'No, you are not bad, but it is bad to beg.' Even as I said it I heard history laughing at me.

We walked on, towards the Norfolk. He was a Christian, he said, as if reopening negotiations, and his Christian name was Boniface. Suppose he came to England, would there be a job for him? ... I got him to read me the names on shops. We came to the Norfolk and he said, with his curiously histrionic sadness, 'Oh, I help you to come here and—'

And I went in and sat drinking beer on the terrace, and he slowly walked past, up and down, up and down, until at last he tired and I saw him no more. And inside me I was saying, in gloomy celebration of my failure to master or even clearly to understand the situation (which anyone with a touch of worldliness, and that included all my fellow-guests at the Norfolk, would have seen through at once): Damn, damn, damn, damn, damn ...

4

At breakfast I had what wasn't quite grapefruit—and a ring of pineapple—and did not have porridge, bacon, various sorts of omelette, black pudding, cereals familiar and bizarre, and innumerable varieties of fruit, all offered.

And to Broadcasting House: to be interviewed by a young

producer, white, who began by asking me what I hoped to contribute during my stay in Kenya; a question that called forth my defensive modesty at its most intricate. I made a good case for my not being there at all, and the question had to be asked, and answered, again.

From there I went to see an old friend I'd known as a poet in London—a chuckling student, too, but who now, back at home, was an administrator in an important position. Willy had written gentle poems in which he appeared to be breaking his heart over the beauty of certain very English flowers. I'd always been confident that these poems, in their delicate mawkishness, constituted travesties of feelings that, in Willy's native Kikuyu (and given flowers more African), would have appeared fairly robust. I'd met him at the official opening of Book Week, when he'd disclosed, obliquely but unmistakeably, that his poems were now concerned with the beggars to be found in every doorway in Nairobi.

But when I met him in his office in the city, it was a very different Willy. I didn't realise this immediately, and greeted him with the boisterous familiarity that had become habitual between us. Willy did not reply in kind. Suddenly he was stiff and uneasy with importance. 'Willy!' I cried. 'Good to see you at home!' He replied, after a chill moment, in the manner of someone interviewing a probably bogus candidate for academic honours, 'What do you think of Professor J. H. Walsh's *The Use of the Imagination?*' I wondered, very much taken aback (and feeling horridly like Falstaff at the end of *Henry IV, Part II*), if it was one of those embarrassments that arose out of linguistic abruptnesses. The wife of a Kikuyu I'd befriended in England had sent to *my* wife, out of the blue, a small woven basket. The accompanying note simply said: 'Have this little bag.' Half the problems of the world, it had sometimes occurred to me (following such experiences and the whole example of my BBC programme), might spring from differences in tone between languages; between, especially, the naturally laconic tongues, of which Kikuyu seemed to be one, and those that are more effusive.

But no. Willy was signalling to me the fact that he was no longer the apprentice of his London days. He was now, under the age of thirty, a power in the land ...

Simply faced with his immaculateness of dress (the starch

of his manner aside), I felt a tramp. But in that heat, I couldn't bring myself to assume the absurd suit, the wildly inappropriate necktie.

And that afternoon, in the hall where the main events of Book Week were to occur, I heard about Willy's problem from Tom Mboya. He gave a lecture on the relationship between Kenya's ruling political party and the intellectual. He had those curious rhetorical gifts, matters of timing and phrasing—*theatrical* matters—that make their possessor an irresistibly compelling speaker. Africa, he said, was much bothered at this moment by the problems of the educated man—or the intellectual. 'Perhaps one day we shall be able to afford to distinguish between the two.' Indeed, it was an *enormous* African dilemma: that all its intellectuals (or educated men and women) were now of the same age: and so many must reconcile themselves to spending their working lives at the second or third, or at an even lower, level. It was a great awkwardness, said this bright, doomed man. So large a proportion of Africans were becoming Ph.Ds. 'But'—he stared along a vista of indiscriminate reputations not unlike those that plagued the new African literature—'there are Ph.Ds ... and Ph.Ds.' The hall fell about with appalled delight.

In the audience was a European acquaintance of mine who worked under my friend Willy. He often, she said, didn't know what was going on. He had made her aware that one of the gifts of the administrator was simply that of keeping abreast of affairs inside the organisation he helps to administer. Willy seemed to go out of his way to avoid having such knowledge. He made sudden decisions that reduced whole schemes to nonsense; each time having, it was clear, reminded himself abruptly that the making of a decision, no matter what, was the mark of the administrator. Willy was the one person they could talk to—much of him being the old Willy of his days as student and trainee in London, but he was also capable, having been intimate and reassuring, of walking through a door and instantly becoming distant and dismaying.

I thought, roughly, on the basis of the day's experience, that it was like being in a school after the pupils had taken over. There was that wide range of embarrassments that would result. Walter Ellis had said that morning, about a reception to be given for my fellow novelist and myself, 'Not many Africans invited, I'm afraid. But there aren't many at this level, you know. They stand about and are embarrassed.'

It seemed to me that there was only one logical view of this situation: that embarrassment is psychologically fatiguing, and that to endure it equably you needed guts—but that it was only in the enduring of embarrassment that the answer lay. There had surely to be an attempt to fight through to understanding, and simply to comfortable relationships; and the attempt couldn't begin too soon. As it was, you smiled, and as often as not the answer was a blankness, reflecting any of a wide range of responses, from feelings of inferiority to those of aggressive suspicion.

It was necessary, I thought, not to turn the other cheek, but to lose the other face. All round there must be the most cheerful willingness to lose all the faces that there were to be lost.

I'd much liked Willy's friendly face, and would have been happy to see him lose, nay quite energetically cast away, his cold important one. And of course, since I must have some face that stood in the way of understanding, let me lose that too.

I remembered an African novel that had attempted to describe what it was like, hopelessly young, to take over the role of the vanished colonial official, to sit at the desk that the man himself had sat at only yesterday, with such confidence, and to engage in what turned out to be act after act of uneasy imitation. Even the life of the city, and of the official living in the city, came unnaturally. It made sense enough if you had centuries of Western individualism behind you, but behind the hero of the novel, as behind my old friend Willy, stretched a long village tradition, the fruit of a view of life that was the very reverse of individualistic.

And the poor man, the official in the story, defeated in a task he cannot make his own, reflects that back in the village you could be as unfortunate as anywhere else in the world, but at least, there, your misfortune would become the common concern. You would not be left to fall to pieces in any parody of splendour such as the city offered.

68

5

There were rough relationships in the British Council office, too. Walter, not entirely recognisable, said to an assistant, 'You seem full of trite sayings today.' They both smiled at me as if to persuade me that the appearance of a quarrel was an appearance, merely. 'I am glad that I bore you,' said the other to Walter, directing at me an even wider smile. I smiled back and, all smiling, we drove to a school for children saved from the streets. We gave books. Walter spoke, with his real kindness, and I spoke after him, feeling deeply unnecessary. It was as if old Mother Hubbard, when she went to the cupboard, had had an assistant to duplicate her benevolent actions. We drove back, all scowling, and Walter took me out towards Lake Naivasha. Vivid red earth; bright people; women hoeing, babies on their backs; sudden swarms of little girls in gaily green school clothes. Walter had friends with him, on holiday in Kenya. The man was an old schoolfellow, and Walter whispered that he'd married his wife out of kindness. Her headaches were strategic, not real. She knew he'd been merely kind, and was always punishing him with her pains, and general vapourishness. She was generally vapourish as we drove back to Nairobi in the warm failing light. Walter smiled and scowled together; and it all seemed a terrible warning against ever being kind.

Should Swahili be the National Language? was then discussed, a Book Week event. The speakers had obviously locked horns in this matter many times: a linguist, a biologist, an official of the Ministry of Education. They made monstrous fun of each other, and seemed at one point to be debating the propriety —or, strictly speaking, the impropriety—of telling, in one language or the other, blue jokes. I ended up, quite to my astonishment, in favour of Swahili, a language of which I

69

knew nothing except that it had difficulty in accommodating modern scientific terms.

‹ I had the feeling I'd had several times already, of a nation comporting itself much like some very alert small town.

But then a publisher's cocktail party. It was like one of those London parties familiar to me, but exiled. It was full of yearning for London. Having no yearning of the kind myself, I was glad to be rescued by Colin, who took me to see a bad African play, worse acted. We crept away, and I confessed my longing to escape from the hotel, and Colin said that was easy, I must simply come and stay with him.

How, I wondered, did I ever come to be on this slope of grass, in glaring sunlight, blinking at the hundred boys —some of them fairly elderly boys—who were sitting cross-legged, waiting for me to speak? Over sky-blue shirts they wore red blazers. The slope ran down from the school grounds straight into the valley, where the village was. The valley was red, too. So was the narrow road by which we'd come to it, and the hedges that lined the road were red with dust. And everywhere were clumps of poinsettia, a weed, blood-red.

I felt like an export version of my old schoolmastering self.

They'd given me a kind of ... conducted tour of their writing. Well, it had been spread out on tables in one of the schoolrooms, and we'd walked round it. All, it turned out, detective stories. One I half-read under the anxious eye of its creator: The Hexagonal Murders. Bodies had been found littered all over Nairobi, a hexagonal pattern of bullet holes in their foreheads. Brooding on the curious geometry of these crimes (and perhaps on the commodious brows of the victims), the hero went to a restaurant and ordered tea.

'He was halfway through when he lifted the biscuit tray to put it aside. In doing so he felt an object under the tray. He lifted the tray to see what it was. There, under the tray, was an attached envelope addressed to him! Detaching it, he opened it and took out a white unruled paper, very thin. On it was typed a message to him. Before opening it he looked round, trying to notice if anybody was taking particular interest in him. He noticed no one. With fingers not too hasty he opened the folded paper and read:

Hello, Inspector,

It will be very hard for you to have the points of a hexagon marked on your head with bullets from a gun, so keep wise, Mr Wise, and lay off the hexagonal murders case and those that will come in the same name.

Signed, The Hexagonal Murderers.'

How had the letter been attached to the biscuit tray? I asked the author. Well, someone had crept in, pretending to be a waiter, he said, and had then made a quick getaway by car. A strangely complicated and perilous way of delivering such a note? He grinned, and I felt a prig to have made the point. It was taken by them all to be essential to such stories that neither side should behave with reference to common sense.

And here I was, required to talk about writing to what had turned out to be a regiment of young crime novelists. The tree I was sitting under, I now noticed, was aflame with red flower. A dozen small children ran across the bottom of the valley below, dressed in explosive scraps of orange, bright blue, brighter green. A bird landed at my feet, opened its wings so that I should be in no doubt that it had been individually designed by Matisse in one of his less sober moods, and flew away with the cry of someone who'd just avoided being made a victim of the Hexagonal Murderers.

Well, as a writer, I said, I had been excited and astounded by the colours of the valley they lived in. A writer spent much of his life wondering what words he'd use for the things around him, and at the back of my mind I'd been struggling with the problem of describing the valley's astonishing base of redness without using the word 'red' over and over again, but also without obtrusively using other words for 'red'. Or perhaps the way *was* to use the word 'red' over and over again? What did they think? The point was that here was I, a stranger, to whom the features of the world they lived in, commonplace to them, were totally amazing. Quite frankly, I didn't believe the flowers over my head were so red! Nor the earth at my feet! Earth couldn't be so red! And this absurd illusion of perpetual sunshine! The marvellous but quite imaginary blue of the sky! 'You made it all up just before I came,' I said. 'Admit it! You painted things ... *that* red—*that* green—*that* yellow! You did it to deceive me!'

71

I'd enjoyed their detective stories, but what I'd like to read were their accounts of the world about us, their everyday world, which to me was so improbable. I'd like to have stories of theirs to take home, that would convince my friends who also lived in the pale world of the North that such places existed as this valley, inhabited by such people as themselves. Would they write such stories and send them to me in London?

Once again I distributed books.

6

Events were now not so much following fast upon one another as fusing together. So there was—or the timetable vowed that there'd been—a symposium of African writing of which I could remember nothing—except that I'd said (had I?) that at the moment African writing had two needs, awkwardly contradictory: that of encouragement, and that of critical severity. There'd been cocktails—but there were always cocktails—and perhaps, at one of these, my requiring a Hungarian diplomat to recite 'To be or not to be' in his own tongue? If that was uncertain, there was no uncertainty about having been in hot cars travelling the hot city to present more books. Cocktails again—and again—and that reception for my fellow-writer and myself, largely attended by expatriates who talked about everything but books and writing.

Expatriates! *Expats,* they were called, fondly or furiously. It seemed to me that many were professional exiles … people, that is, whose calling was to be away from home. They were enormously drawn to living elsewhere than in Britain. Well, much human achievement rested on such things as Francis Drake's anxiety to absent himself from Devon. But this condition of being a professional expatriate rested on a special desire—didn't it?—not to have to create a domestic existence for oneself. And it was, I thought, very often a bad basis for being abroad as a representative of the people at home. It was like stick-in-the-muds being represented by flibbertigibbets.

There was the pretended interest in the cross-pollination of cultures, or political systems, and the actual interest in escape. Or a deep longing for the exotic. And I was beginning to see, or to believe that I saw—and some of this had rubbed off from ten years of African literature—that there was danger in putting yourself in the position of viewing the world as, fundamentally, an exotic place.

Fundamentally (I thought in this blazing, brilliant Kenya), it was a *homely* place.

There was that column of ebony that stood in the fireplace in Colin's bungalow, where I was now living. The work of those great Tanzanian wood-carvers, the Makonde. The old and young, the men and women and children, the dead and living, swarming up the column, and over the top, and down the other side, in a tangle of hands held, legs clutched, limbs deviously knitted to limbs, a carved chain of existence that stretched through the world of the dead and back again into the world of the living, and defied the very notion of separateness, loneliness—or annihilation. It made me think of the boys and men I'd seen walking through Nairobi hand in hand.

It made me think also of my father, since it was such a long way from his desolate feeling about death as one's being sent brutally out of the room for ever.

In the British Council office it was much as in school staff rooms I'd known. Morning coffees, grunted remarks, in-jokes: and Walter Ellis saying, 'You've reported every day, and given yourself a very full programme.' I felt astoundingly satisfactory. But I noticed that none of them ever came to the occasions in which I was involved. Not to the symposiums, or the visits to the display of books—which were indeed far out of the physical reach of the bewildered schoolchildren brought to view them—or the meetings with writers.

Well, I was glad of that last. I met my friends largely at Colin's. James, the novelist, though he was on the point of abandoning the name in favour of the one he might have had if missionaries had never existed, was as shy as ever he'd been at Leeds or in London, boy-like, a grin. He was still, when you spoke to him, like a lizard, rather; there was the quick scuttle of something darting to cover. That feeling you always had on meeting him again, of an evasive, scuttling boy with a large grin! And then you saw how wrong it was; you suddenly were aware of his sulking power, which sulked because so much around him was trivial. That effect of scuttling was really an angry flinching from a smooth world. He was an angry man, full of spears. The boy was a towering man, with no gift for boyish games. It was many of the men around him who were boys, *playing* at African writing.

He'd written nothing since the novel that had been so subtle about the struggle for independence, in which he'd been drawn into an examination of the very notion of heroism—in the end perhaps no one was ever a hero! It was a story full of the agony and injury of that struggle—for both black and white. In its last pages the novel had looked anxiously towards the new world of independence. *Would* it be a new world—a world renewed?

The anger you felt in him sprang from his not finding it renewed, at all ...

And I was glad to go with a solitary teacher to a school for crippled children, whose legs had become useless in a host of twisted ways, and who by a host of different obstinacies of motion made their way to us, and clutched at *our* legs, and hung on and laughed in the sheer delight of being visited. Their vitality seemed ten times that of any group of uncrippled people, anywhere. And across the red road to the primary school that had been knocked together by the people of the neighbourhood, on the self-help principle, a collection of leaning loose boxes; and teachers looking grinning out of the open stable door of what, in chalk, proclaimed itself as the staff room; and the crowded classes, light streaming in through knotholes, dark faces in the darkness teased by moths of light, and a teacher writing on the blackboard, with enormous slowness and enormous inaccuracy, the word 'metamorphosis' ...

And, by way of sufficiently astonishing contrast, to the highest-flying school of them all, a sort of tropical Winchester.

Below there was an immense flatness of mud, cracked with

streams, and enormous shadow. The wheels of the little aeroplane had gone up into their case, with an effect oddly insect-like. I was in a throbbing beetle in clouds above Africa. 4400 miles—and two weeks and a day—from home. Next stop: Entebbe.

Oh the constant interested exhaustion! I'd never been so fascinated and so weary! Ordeal by heat and glare!—and scarcely endurable novelty of experience!—and cocktails! Yesterday, the red twisting road to Machakos, and beyond, to a training college for teachers and primary school run by White Fathers. Little children in scraps of dress staring from hedges, in the company of their goats; in odd places, gypsy circles of men and women. And we'd come to this plateau quietly occupied by buildings, and were met by Father O'Riordan, calm-faced and smiling, with a straw hat on the back of his head. There were two other Fathers, with a general level of good looks remarkably above the average. I was taken aback to find three Irishmen so handsome in such a place.

Father O'Riordan had taken me across to the school. Outside, a tree with a child's luncheon packet hanging from every branch. And in the first room, this enchanting girl—oh, such unlikelihood of loveliness everywhere!—whose name, the last even the most unromantic speculator would have guessed, was Sister Scholastica. She was rehearsing the children in that well-known Kenyan nursery rhyme, Tinker, Tailor. . . . Father O'Riordan said, 'Our visitor comes from London. Where is London, children?' The children chorussed, 'London is the capital of Ireland, Father.' Father O'Riordan blushed, and drew my attention to the half of the classroom floor that was covered with a model, in clay, of nothing less than the city of Nairobi. Indeed, of much more than the city of Nairobi, for in the shadows to this side and that I found the airport, full of planes with drooping wings, and the National Park, which had room only for a few representative and extremely approximate animals: a sort of lion that must, on that scale, have been fifty feet long, and a kind of giraffe one hundred feet tall. The very dust seemed to grin in the room. Sister Scholastica smiled, and my heart leapt in a fashion unprovided for by Walter Ellis's timetable. Father O'Riordan, who wore his straw hat like a tatty halo, gently led me away.

To the priests' house, then, for one of the most talkative lunches I'd ever experienced. The room seemed full of bottles of beer and cigarettes, and it couldn't be denied that the Fathers had a sort of ... unworldly worldliness. It appeared to be epitomised—though thinking this was perhaps the effect of the beer and all that holy smoke—by the enormous boots visible under their cassocks. Had we, they asked first and wistfully, any Rugby news? Our blank faces made them sigh, and then smile to cancel out the sighs. Well, then. I was a literary man. So was ... Brendan Behan. A man (they sighed again) of shocking worldliness. What had I to tell them—in lieu of Rugby gossip—about Brendan Behan? Details of his worldliness were clearly welcome.

We lunched immensely, care being taken that, if a great dish of roast beef left us empty, the failure of hospitality might be put right by the even larger dish of roast chicken. And Father Riley talked to me about the problems of teaching English to his teachers-in-training. 'How,' he asked, 'would you make clear to them the difference between "creep" and "crawl"?'

And we went to the library, which contained an almost complete set of G.A. Henty, among many Victorian novels and mildewed school stories of a lachrymose kind. The Fathers had made this collection—which must have stamped their young charges with a lifelong tendency to lag a century or so behind the rest of the world—by the expenditure of a few pennies at a time in the rag-and-bone-and-book shops of Nairobi.

And once again I presided over a gift of books.

Back in the British Council office, Walter Ellis said, 'You've been a very easy and accommodating visitor.' Which made me wish, not for the first time, for a touch of my father. If only, once, someone would say how difficult, how dreadfully unco-operative I had been.

7

Henry Smythe made me wish this wish again, rather more vehemently.

He did not care for Africa. Africa, it was at once clear as he drove me from the airport, was occupied by a mass of undifferentiated humanity, for whom the word was 'they'. 'They've been noisy all night,' he said of the inhabitants of the Ugandan capital. 'They don't care,' he said, as a cheerful public works lorry went past with more wheels on one side than on the other.

His natural home was in any of the ancient seats of European civilisation. He was an exiled exile, an expatriated expatriate.

If he was averse to African humanity, he was peculiarly angered by African plant life. In his garden—he showed it to me almost instantly on our arrival—grew a ginger lily. Misled by the name, suggestive of some prim European flower, he'd thrown a seed in the ground close to the house. Within minutes, as he told the story, there was this grossly sexual vegetable extruding vast bulbs and, as it were, overground tubers: a four-letter plant. It was indulging, he seemed to think, somewhere in the middle of the violently colourful, insolently odorous wigwam it made, in activities so disgusting that, if you stood and listened (but he wouldn't do that; virtually he stopped his ears, when near it), you'd hear erotic guffaws, a brutal uproar of vegetable ravishments.

There were, too, his moon flowers. About these, because an un-African element of precise timing was involved, he was less severe. 'If you care to come out on the verandah a few seconds before six-twenty,' he said on my first evening, 'you will see something rather remarkable. Yes—I think, a little out of the way.' I came out at 6.19 and at 6.20, as the

77

temperature dropped by one degree, the moonflowers, which all day had hung furled amid their trellis-supported foliage, like large versions of the twiddled corner of handkerchief my mother would insert into my nostril when I was a child, gave little shudders and shook themselves open ... very much as another sort of handkerchief, tightly folded for the pocket, might be shaken open. Each flower would shiver and twitch itself into an enormous white plate, a disc so fragrant that you recoiled. It was a fragrance quite profoundly impolite—to a European nose, aggressively excessive. Difficult, nostrils full of it, to go in again with Smythe and respond to his dry, measured remarks, or listen to his wistful talk of Europe. 'You know that part of the Auvergne?' But your mind was entirely fixed on this part of Africa.

My hopes of rescue, which in Kenya had rested on Colin, rested here on my friend Robert, who taught literature at Makerere.

I hadn't expected to need rescue in either country, but in both the necessity of it became quickly clear. Otherwise I'd be trapped in a world inset in Africa, and largely insulated from it. As was proved my first evening in Kampala, when I was taken to a party at the British High Commission. I was introduced to people who reacted quite nastily to the perfectly ordinary fact that they'd never heard of me. It was an offence for me to be present, which implied a state of having been heard of, and yet be actually ... unheard of. One very pretty girl positively laughed at my predicament. 'And *what* are you here for?' 'It's called a Book Week.' She laughed even more loudly before abruptly leaving me. Clearly she'd never known a week to be given a more absurd title.

I thought back to a party in London, when a fellow guest had asked 'Who are you?'—quite brutally, as if my being anyone at all was an offence. I named myself. 'Oh,' he said, his voice burrowing into the party buzz. 'I hear you talking about art on BBC3, don't I?' 'No. Not me.' 'Every month. Or is it quarterly?' 'Must be someone who sounds like me.' 'Oh yes, I think I quite liked your last talk. Can't remember what it was about. I *think* I liked it.' 'Quite unqualified to talk about art,' I said. 'Interesting. Wish I could remember what you were discussing.' If it had really been me, as he seemed to think, then I was clearly the person to ask about this. But he

78

appeared to regard my being myself as a positive disqualification when it came to establishing facts about myself. I felt scandalously unindentifiable.

As I did at the British High Commission's party.

But now came Robert—an instant object of Henry Smythe's suspicion. Well, Robert wore African shirts, and had a general air of being some sort of honorary African. We sat in the garden briefly, and Robert pointed out to me the huge purple phallic seedboxes of banana plants growing there: and I could see that they were, to Henry Smythe, simple confirmations of his worst feelings about Africa. Africa would come, in its boiling hot, laughing way, and impregnate you and make you bear hideous flowers or fruit.

Robert had been a transmitter of much of the writing that reached our programme from East Africa. He was a man of apparently unlimited energy, always engaged on half a dozen incompatible tasks at once. Now he snatched me up and drove me round Kampala, up and down its hills—exclaiming as we went at this spectacle or that, discussing students whose work I knew, outlining new courses he was preparing for them, filling in the cracks of his discourse with a history of the city. Suddenly he braked and was out of the car, talking to someone with a bundle under his arm. 'Laban! I'm so glad to see you!' And I realised that I'd known this tired Laban well, back at the BBC. He was a poet who'd come to London to be trained as a broadcaster. 'We heard you were in prison,' said Robert. 'I was,' said Laban. 'But they've just let me out.'

He'd been accused, he told us, of being involved in a plot to oust the President. And their proof? he'd demanded. They had perfect proof, they said. A spy had been present at meetings of the conspirators, and had taken secret photographs. Laban was clearly to be seen in these. They'd gone away then and fetched the photographs to show him how hopelessly cornered he was, and he wasn't there. He wasn't to be seen, when they looked carefully, in any of the photographs at all. So they'd let him go.

I smiled my helpless old-friend-from-London's smile at this character out of political melodrama, and we drove on. 'I don't know,' I said, 'that I could bear to live here. It's like living in the French Revolution. I mean—Laban. He's a *poet!*' I caught myself speaking as if being a poet was a protection against political nastiness, and realised that much of me believed it was. And Shakespeare's Casca—torn for his bad verses?

'Don't,' said Robert, 'be a prig. This isn't London, you know.' He gestured at the extremely un-Londonish city that flowed past us, aflame with blossoming trees. 'There's a lot of sorting out to do. There's a lot of getting things right. It's not the same year here as it is at home, you know.'

I thought, not for the first time, that being British, having rested your life on the belief that it was safe to walk almost anywhere at any time of day, and that no special danger offered itself in the vicinity of the Houses of Parliament—that being British was almost a disqualification for being a citizen of the world.

8

Book Week in Kampala was short of something—almost certainly, efficiency. Main events tended to take place in inaccessible buildings, and a speaker might find himself separated from his audience by several miles. There was a general air of constraint; it was a politically awkward moment, the air whispering of coups. I found the city beautiful but sinister.

In Robert's flat on the university campus I met his one-time chauffeur, Noah, who had taken to drawing. One day he'd seen someone at work with wax crayons, and had asked to be allowed to attempt this strange activity himself. He drew instantly an astonishing picture of a mother with her baby; he sprawled sensuously across her bosom; huge eyes, penis, legs spread in the happiness of being legs; she, huge eyes also, immense lips, breasts. Merely the design it made held you across Robert's room, before you saw what it was. He'd gone on drawing; had now a mountain of work. Robert went away to fetch students; Noah, he said, would show me what he'd done. The heavy sheets were heaped on a table. More huge-eyed children sprawling in the laps of their mothers. Girls dreaming: their dreams, crayoned hazes in the background—handsome teachers, usually. Boys dreaming —of lovers who might have been teachers, sisters, mothers. Someone drank out of a gourd, through a straw, and it was beautiful and wicked. The long-horned cattle Noah drew were people, too. A bull with lowered eyes brooded among cows. Someone, at Noah's request, had printed out a title: 'Who shall I choose?' All flesh called to all flesh. Any living creature might love any living creature. As he turned one drawing over to reveal another, Noah murmured, explanatorily: 'Love!' The next: 'Love!' His voice grew dreamier, softer, more liquid, like his eyes. His slender hands turning paper. '*Love!*' My senses swam. This world, bright and coloured beyond my northern imagination—this chattering, whistling, roasting world—with this voice at its centre murmuring: 'Love! Love!' It seemed an eroticism not in any way willed or worked up ... but an absolutely natural eroticism, an inevitable aspect of the brightness, the colour, the steady, reliable roasting of things.

Dammit, yes. The sun did tell a different story from the story told by the clouds. We needed dictionaries, not merely of words, but of sensations.

I had to shake my northern wits together, thank Noah, and listen while, on his five-stringed instrument of cactus wood, with burnt decoration, he accompanied himself (it was a ringing of small bells) in a song which he said was devoted to me. I smiled cautiously throughout, wondering if it was serenade or satire.

And Robert brought students back to the flat, the first of a fortnight's flood of them; young men and women, shyly sincere. Here, I thought, my instinct in respect of paper Africa confirmed by the Africa of flesh-and-blood—here literature was still magic: was still needed: wasn't blasé, wasn't a posture.

Well, here was Lydia, neat and shy, in her last year as an honours student of English, the author of a number of terrifying stories based on some of the fiercer customs of her people.

Robert suggested that I move in with him rather than go to the hotel that had been arranged. Henry Smythe said, all right: it would mean longer journeys for the official cars taking me to Book Week events, but never mind ...

But first to judge an essay competition, the entrants being local school children. The subjects would have been familiar to the victims of the most conservative British examination boards: there wasn't a shade of Africanness in any of them, and it was very much on the level of an invitation to agree that the British poets of the first third of the nineteenth century might, on the whole, be described as romantics. Reading with distress what had plainly been produced in distress, I felt it was an undeserved delight when I discovered a reference to 'the great poet Milsworth.' The context did not suggest a satirical intention. I paused in my judging for a while, thinking of other helpless fabrications of the same quality: the playwright Sherispeare, the novelist Dickeray.

And then to Mbale, one hundred and fifty miles to the east. It was an awkward moment to travel: there was impatience with the Kenyans, which had taken the form of beating them over the head at the border, and the British were out of favour; there was talk of road blocks and ill-controlled Army activity in that corner of the country. Henry Smythe urged my driver at all costs to stop when challenged, and answer military questions calmly. The official car must not be endangered. He advised me, I thought with some pleasurable gloom, to make myself small in the back seat.

It was a beautiful road. High Street, Africa, I thought. An immense amount of cycling—many bicycles seeming to be ridden by bananas. There was, certainly, a human being somewhere among the tall green stacks of fruit that climbed from handlebars and saddles. Sometimes there was much more than a human being: there were what looked like entire families. There were wives and aunts and children. But even then, the banana was dominant.

There were red-brown mud huts and shelters of pole and thatch where men and women lay or listened to huge radios or washed their hair. And there was the forest. It was the first total forest I'd seen, in which the new growth climbed on the old and became old itself, and was climbed upon, and all was made by creepers into tottering parcels of greenstuff. I sought earnestly for a word to describe all this, and arrived at last at 'impenetrable.' Then I knew that I was very tired indeed.

There was one road-block only, and then I was in Mbale; and at once back in Britain, round about 1936, for my host, the friendliest man, had mannerisms that had become museum pieces at home. I reflected how impossible it was in Britain any longer to lace what one said with such emphatics as 'frightfully' and 'extraordinarily'. It was ... extraordinarily strange to hear English so English in a part of Africa so African. Almost at once I was being driven into hills, and was delivering a lecture. Outside the lecture room there was a pool, and the pool was populated by bullfrogs. I was astonished that creatures so tiny, working together, could produce so great a noise. They were the tiny authors of collective thunder. They'd have drowned my talking—especially since my voice now was only a shred of itself. So my host took on the task of bullfrog-quietener. He stood by the pool and every time a bullfrog filled its pouch with air, ready to roar, he beat the surface of the water with a stick: which brought about startled deflation ... I talked about the emergence of African writing, but thought about the silencing of African bullfrogs.

And in the morning, *frightfully* early, we made our way along a road called, for some reason, the taxi route. It was no more than a narrow red path, wrapped in greenness. Everywhere, small red huts standing in the thrillingly bright green caves made by banana leaves. The air, so early, had a quality as if it had been beaten to transparency out of mother-of-pearl. You could smell the stillness. I wondered dizzily at my presence there, in a place so beautiful, in such plummily anecdotal company, on my way to ... Well, it turned out to be a school, where I spoke much of the morning until I was hoarse. The headmaster was Asian, a little explosive ball of a man, who told me of a problem that was on his mind. A boy living two hundred miles away had been given a place in the school, starting the following term. Yesterday he'd arrived, weeks before he'd been told to, having walked and hitched his way from home. He'd come so early because he was afraid if he didn't actually occupy the place he'd been given, it might turn out not to exist. Or someone else might occupy it.

83

What should they do? Send him home again? Too cruel. Keep him? Too rash: because then everyone would come early ...

Back in my host's house, I slept intensely, waking to a marvellous night: starlight so strong you could still see the colours of things, and suddenly a wind that made the house shiver. It promised rain, to general delight; but, to general chagrin, withheld it.

These strange Ugandan weathers! A few nights before, I'd sat with Robert on the patio of a bungalow belonging to one of his colleagues, surrounded by the hot-cross-bun coiffures of the little girls of the house, when a thunderstorm had taken place on the horizon; far off, a perfectly self-contained event, like some distant battle fought with swords, noisily inaudible, and with no reference at all to the unruffled air above us ...

My host's daughter swung on the lintels of doors, was in love with an American and talked American ('Right!'), was at the beginning of everything, in her slightness quite unafraid of the world, even given alarmingly to teasing it ... and in the morning, barefoot, drove me to the market. I'd never known mornings like these in Mbale; they were the quintessence of the very idea of a morning: the world refreshed, the air infinitely delicate. In the market they were selling paraffin lamps made out of old tins, fish dried till they were mere blacknesses, peanuts in twirls of graph paper, and the most mysterious odds and ends—the shattered remains of a kingfisher, a snake skin, shredded leaves.

Then, in the official car, in which I felt like a stowaway, to a girls' school given and built by the American Government. It was designed to educate the future wives of future Ministers, senior officials, men generally of importance, and to that end offered luxury in every department. The domestic science rooms were stuffed with expensive machinery, the library with expensive books, the art rooms with paintings reproduced by the best processes. I spoke to a hundred or so glowing girls in gym slips. Their presence seemed no more probable than my own, or than the existence (in that torrid world in which, on every road, children stood begging for money for their school fees) of this totally American building.

By a guidance counsellor out of the States for the first time, who'd fallen helplessly in love with Africa, I was taken on a tour of the school, from the tall bell-tower of imported stone to her own living room, which was circular ('Lovely—but they never thought of the problem with bookshelves'). She'd concluded already that her specific connection with the continent, as a member of the staff of a school for important wives, was fragile. How could being an important wife be the object of any education? she had come to ask herself. But if being a guidance counsellor in Eastern Uganda didn't last as a reason for being in Africa, and she feared it wouldn't, she'd have to find other reasons for staying.

9

There were explosions in the night and a clatter of machine-gun fire: then the sound of excited chatter. A rather horrid sort of dawn chorus. It was like sleeping on the edge of a 'B' film. I fell asleep again and dreamt that I was wandering among wars. It was the end of the world, but the world was Mbale—was beautiful, an endless post-human morning in caves created out of banana leaves. . . . At breakfast Robert's cook, John, said there were many bodies in the streets in one of the quarters of Kampala. He described the scene in some detail, a clearly observant and reliable eye-witness. Well, how could there be anything vague about a man who ironed my underwear until it seemed too exquisite, in terms of the creases it fell into, to be worn?

John's story turned out, all the same, to be totally untrue. The night's melodrama dwindled to a rumour of inter-regimental rivalries in one of the barracks. But the President did not open Book Week, as had been arranged ...

When I returned from lectures, events that did not occur, or occurred in some other place than where I was, lunches, cocktail parties, Robert provided me with students to see, on the basis of stories and poems they had written—with which he also provided me. The flow of writers and their work was adjusted to the unusual notion of a day of, perhaps, thirty-six hours. Cheerfully filling my arms with manuscripts, Robert would dash off to attend a dozen board meetings, conduct half a dozen seminars, rearrange the lives of three or four students. He wouldn't, I'd surely understand, be back for quite an hour or so. Meanwhile, Jared, Yusuf, Mary and Taban would be in to see me half an hour from now. It looked, Robert admitted (wryly, and with the surprise of someone unaccustomed to peering so far ahead) as if we'd be eating at midnight. Or even later. Oh, some broadcasting chaps would be looking in after that. They'd talk about that discussion to be recorded tomorrow when I'd be joined in the studio by Ocol, Sam, Timothy, Stella—or it might be Okello, David, Emma and Joseph. Where the devil was his clean shirt? And would I like to glance at his notes on Ben Jonson's *Bartholomew Fair?* Hadn't said he'd been asked to prepare a new edition of that? Would be very interested to have my views on the play itself and the general tendency of his critical commentary. Might fit that in some time today, or very early tomorrow, ha ha, because he really had to send something off to the publisher in the UK not later than the morning post.

'All go,' said Robert, then, enclosing the vulgar phrase in more sets of quotation marks than I could count. He had the literary academic's habit, I thought fondly and exasperatedly, of regarding the whole of life, including everyday conversation, as editable matter. His madly busy existence was a hubbub of footnotes.

We were together for a meeting of the Kampala Writers' Group, at which I was a guest of honour. I said how much, as someone who cared for the English language, I looked forward to the development of African English. In the 'thirties in Britain, when I was at school, there'd been a wave of—largely episcopal—rage caused by the arrival of Americanisms. Character-rotting usages such as 'Sez you', 'Oh yeah', 'O.K.' It was our English master who'd mocked this verbal prudery ('Do you know what they call dancing-pumps? *High-shine hop-shoes!*' His face glowing with pleasure). I looked forward, I said, to renewed outbursts among opponents of innovation, directed against a flood of Africanisms.

'Ah,' said a courteous Bugandan, 'ah, no!' He must take the liberty of disagreeing. Well, suppose that he wished to invite a friend to his home after this meeting. What he would say, alas—how awful to have to confess it!—was 'Come to mine'. Now, there was a vile invention for you! One that made it plain that the only safety lay in using the guaranteed English of those guaranteed to be English.

Which was still capable of unorthodoxies, I protested. And his example seemed to me to pass the tests of acceptable language: it was attractive, and its meaning was in no doubt.

We exchanged unconvinced smiles.

Increasingly I felt that I was regarded as an official visitor who'd gone native. The focus of this view was provided not only by my decision to lodge with Robert, substantially in Africa, rather than in a hotel, substantially out of it, but also by my relations with the poet Kota, who had recently been appointed director of the National Theatre. He wanted British culture to vacate its quarter of the building, on the public grounds that, since under his direction the theatre would be given over to African drama and dance, more room was needed for costumes and musical instruments: on the private grounds (so canvassed that they also rapidly became public) that a National Theatre in Uganda belonged to Africa rather than to Europe.

Henry Smythe's attitude surprised me. It was that, if a fight was sought, a fight would be provided. He had no doubt at all that the drama Kota had in mind would consist of 'screeching and screaming'. It would be some sort of village barbarity masquerading as theatrical art. He had no intention of being ousted from the building, or from the particular view of human culture ('tittering and giggling', Kota had been heard to murmur) that he believed it to represent.

As I became more and more aware, it was a clash, again, between a sparkling mischief that happened to be African and a frowning sobriety that, alas, happened not to be. This was given edge by Kota's character, for which, in fact, such a term as 'mischievous' was barely adequate. He'd just published a long poem that was, in essence, an attack on the

87

Westernised ways of the educated African. It expressed carefully wide-eyed and deceptively innocent amazement at such a creature's taste in dress and music, and his attitudes to cooking, time, sickness, death. Totally unpuritanical, it took delight in feigning a puritanical horror of Westernised forms of dance, with their tolerance of actual bodily contact between men and women. Yet the poem, I thought, wasn't really crying out against imported practices because they were in themselves detestable, or foolish. Kota was not intrinsically an opponent of the waltz or the electric stove. Somewhere in the poem there was a declaration: he did not despise the customs of foreigners. But—it was what he was asking—why should they be adopted at the expense of one's own customs?

The poem seemed to me to speak up for a dream. It expressed a longing that people would have respect for the coherence of cultural habit, and would consider carefully the value of their own roots before they dug them up. Wickedly funny, it was a cry of horror—an echo of a cry uttered by many of the most sensitive African writers. And what caused the horror was the easy smashing of the old African world, not only by intrusive Europeans but by their African imitators, and the easy adoption of alien habits.

Kota chose to make it a war between the drum and the piano. One was truly African, the other was not. 'Drum, drum, drum!' he was given to crying: 'not tinkle, tinkle, tinkle!' It did not seem to me that the word 'tinkle' fairly expressed the genius of the piano, but you could see why Kota chose to claim that it did. It was another retort to the view that African drama must amount to no more than caterwauling.

I was with Henry Smythe in the National Theatre building one day when Kota and some friends decided to erect a pole on the green outside. Later they revealed that it was to be the centrepiece for a regular weekend dance, all invited, a village matter reintroduced into the city. Without this explanation of their activity, it was certainly possible to believe that one was witnessing the first step in the building of a scaffold. I can't think Kota was unaware that it would have this appearance. Henry Smythe made a comment that referred, in fact, to the facing of the building—a pierced screen that filtered the strong light. 'If they began throwing things through that,' he said, 'I believe I could dodge two out of three.'

It was absurd, I thought, this division of things into the respectable and the unrespectable. But if it was insisted upon, then I knew which ... disreputable mob I belonged to.

10

The presentation to the President of the first home-grown school textbook; rumoured to be not particularly home-grown, after all. Meetings, expeditions, exhibitions. A British publisher on tour assuring me there'd be no African literature until the emergence of the first African Agatha Christie and Enid Blyton. Talks to everyone capable of being talked to. A meeting with the exiled Kabaka's musicians, who preserved their instruments, and the intricate ceremonies of their music, against the day when their master returned. A wild evening as the guest of a Bugandan writer whose home, he said, halting the hilarity, stood on the spot where the Kabaka's executioners had once been extremely busy. Driving home through the red light district, queues of men at the doors of midnight shacks. I seemed always, among the disreputable though I was, to be in the polite areas of the city—never having more than a glimpse of the vivid lean-to life that surrounded it and leaked into it.

Lunch at the High Commissioner's, where a steward was rebuked for getting the wines in the wrong order—red before white, if it was not white before red.

Drinking with distaste and exhaustion gallons of beer: never was liquid so null. Eructation fought with the need to be eloquent.

At a dinner I sat next to a black American woman, and was startled to realise how different her blackness was from that of the Africans around us. She was so much more American than black. Her very colour seemed to have been printed by another process. On the other side of me sat a white teacher, who contended that all African novels consisted of pages of proverbs. That was all they were—a few thin characters created so that they could swap old saws and not very modern instances. As for Robert: 'Will you tell him that not all the writing done by Africans is first-rate?'

Much about Robert, with his enormous paternal concern for his young writers, did raise a difficult question. Day after day I was stirred, and didn't see how one could fail to be stirred, by the procession of students bringing stories and poems. Everyone in Africa capable of it seemed to be writing. It really was—every conversation with a young writer confirmed it—a deeply felt attempt to control and under- stand tumultuous experience.

And Robert was in the centre of it ... applauding, scatter- ing encouragement ... arranging for broadcasts, the publica- tion of magazines, the making of books ... He'd once invited a writer out from England, to work with the students, and the man had taken against it all; had shut himself away, crying out against so much encouragement, such a general atmos- phere of enthusiasm. Most of these young people, he said, should be told, politely if possible, to stop writing or ... to keep what they wrote to themselves.

I thought that within a general atmosphere of encourage- ment one ought to be as frank as one could be. Frankness enfolded within a general positiveness. It was how I'd thought teaching should be, of any kind. One needed to be propellant and brake. But there were clearly problems at the extreme ends of the situation. There were the simple dangers of over-encouragement and under-encouragement.

One ought perhaps to be at work somewhere in the middle. Throttling no one—especially because you didn't know how even the apparently ungifted might develop ... in the long run you could never be absolutely sure. But also pampering no one.

But such thoughts staggered about my head, now. After nearly four weeks I was barely able to concentrate, and was filled with a shrieking desire to be home. I heard in my head a low cool voice which was that of a totally imaginary character, absurdly unreal: my wife, Kate. As I sat on the grass outside Robert's flat, talking, talking, amid the constant cawing and chittering of birds, with a small hot wind blowing among the red flowers—as I sat in all that splendour and burning profusion, talking to young people for whom I had this bewildered affection, I longed for the low colour, low sounds and cool airs of home.

Oh, I understood Henry Smythe, despite differences of temperament and taste. There were times when the northern creature in me was appalled by this tropical energy, by everything being so noisily out of doors, by the sheer careless fury with which things grew—or, having grown, died in order to become the host of other energetic growths. I had desperate dreams of being very quiet, rather small, and barely visible.

I walked out through a rage of hissing aircraft; it was as if we were surrounded by dragons. The night seemed to be reeling: I certainly was. Why, I wondered, did travel make me speak in nervous subjunctives—extraordinary tenses I never otherwise used or was even much aware of? I'd left an amazed face behind me at passport control.

And Robert's in the bar. The last couple of days in his ruthless company had been constructed, as to things done, like many-tiered sandwiches. I'd run at some point into Henry Smythe, who'd said: 'Overworked! I can see you are! Well, you wouldn't let me organise your life! Can't blame me!' I didn't blame anyone, aware of the strange profit of it all. I'd go home half-dead but crammed full of Africa. During those last two days I'd made recordings for my programme, and talked to three poets and a short story-writer, and conducted an evening of readings and criticism: and been driven to a nightclub by one of my oldest African friends, who was nevertheless not in the least old, a poet and teacher who revealed as we set out that she'd been learning to drive only for a week or so, and turned out not to have profited much from her lessons; so that we ran helplessly towards houses and in the direction of other amazed cars, and I prepared to die within earshot of her beautiful but, in the circumstances, surprising laughter. But we survived, and I got ready to die in the nightclub instead, lit with the lowest of lights, in which dancers circled with crimson slowness, and the tall unsatisfying bottles of beer accumulated, another of

91

those glass forests that I should remember as part of the African landscape. And a friend of Robert's said yes, Robert was popular with the Africans precisely because he was not popular with the establishment. And I thought of the intricacy of establishments I'd encountered on this journey, black and white, and how it had unexpectedly not been possible to avoid a choice between nestling in the places approved by establishments or breaking out of them.

And then my last morning of waking to instant sweatiness; and being taken to the market to buy bark cloth for Kate and a blouse and skirt of equatorial vividness that I knew she'd never wear but would be glad I'd thought she *might* wear. And so to the National Theatre, where my friend of the night before translated and explained the play we saw, which was about the long-drawn-out formalities of a Bugandan wedding: she, with her local honours degree topped up at Leeds, having been so married herself. I was immensely aware of her black knees, and her princess's profile, and the sharply African smell of her, and thought how she must be aware of my ashen quality ... surely I'd become more and more pallid during these weeks? ... and whatever was the smell of a European. Here I was, a friend with a friend against a background of unfriendly history. Oh yes, all those establishments were attempts, black or white, to assert and re-assert the principle of unfriendliness as the central principle of human affairs. (My father's principle, alas!) I felt what I'd so often felt as a teacher: determined friendliness was the answer to all those historical injuries. But how intensely difficult it was ...

And to the launching of Kota's poem—which turned out to be a matter of dancing, in the National Theatre foyer, and Kota insisting on being photographed for *The People* holding my hand (which I thought afterwards was a shot fired in his battle with Henry Smythe—not that I objected to being employed as such a shot); and my fellow-novelist from Britain telling me, as I set out to photograph his entirely characteristic immense feet and, later, his complete Antarctic of a beard, how he'd once photographed Asquith's tongue, across the floor of a London club—that political mouth had been open, and he'd snapped its depths. And it was he (my fellow-novelist) who asked Kota if he'd read us a little of his poem;

92

and Kota did so, a teasing mischief of voice, not to be forgotten. And a visiting academic murmured that Kota's poem was an attempt to put the clock back. There was nothing for Africa to do but to step into the present—that was to say, the present as the West knew it—and thence into the world's corporate choice of a future. And I thought, looking across at where Kota was now jigging, in a manner best described as Afro-Western, with a splendidly beautiful lady who in other circumstances might have been widely acceptable as, say, the Queen of Africa—I thought how odd it was that it was from grinning Kota that the complex challenge of this poem came: the challenge to reconsider the view, which after all was only a view, that man had only one choice of direction, and must always follow whatever path he finds he's on.

And then to a bar, more damned bottles, and farewells, and Kota clasping me to his left shoulder (I was stiff with the unexpectedness of it) and then, with a great laugh, to the right—enjoying, I'm sure, my English unreadiness for this amazing improvement on the handshake.

And so to Entebbe, and this hissing hot machine, already wondering how I'd begin to account for the experience to Kate when we met in eleven hours' time. And then, cramped and sleepless, to London, by way of the curious nothingness of international airports at night, Rome and Frankfurt; concluding that the experience had in fact been, in some ways, simply too big and exciting to have. I remembered a letter a mother had written to me once when I was a teacher, excusing her son's absence from school. They'd all overslept; or, as she put it, 'We overdone it.' Well, I'd overdone it. Converting my paper Africa into flesh-and-blood Africa, I'd overdone it.

And Kate drove me, shivering, away from London Airport, and I asked her how things were, and she burst into tears. And my sons, who'd taken care to come with her, explained that Jim, her father, had died a few hours earlier of a hopeless cancer.

PART THREE

1

It all came out, now. There'd been at least one night-long haemorrhage, which Dorothy was forbidden to report to anyone. Talk on her part about calling a doctor had brought out his worst angers. Jim had a simple view of medicine. Succumb to it, and all was over. 'I don't want them to get their hands on me,' he'd say, as if they were Burkes and Hares to a man. He had this desperate faith that he could go on living so long as he dodged the healers. There'd been so many days in recent months, we saw looking back, when he'd have ... neuralgia, he called it: a pernickety tummy. He'd eaten less and less, and called it queasiness. Dorothy had known, but had not dared to override his veto. No doctors. Never any doctors.

Until the first week of my absence in Africa, when his condition was suddenly so awful that Dorothy acted out of sheer horror. Waiting to be taken to hospital, he said, bitterly, 'I'll not come back. They've got me now. It's the end.' The operation revealed such a hopeless inner mess that they simply sewed him up again and waited. It didn't take long.

But it wasn't, of course, simply that view of doctors as agents of disablement and death—members of some mortal press gang—that made him reluctant to confess to being ill. Or rather, that view rested on deeper habits of the spirit: including a profound habit of impatience with *fussing*. He had a narrowly masculine detestation of that, coupled with a positive scorn for physical degeneration. One ought to be fit and upright. To be unfit was not so much a physical as a moral lapse. It was all part of that quality of his that made him keep his money in a belt round his waist. He hated banks because they looked after what you ought to be manly

97

enough to look after yourself. Health, money, they were his business, no one else's. No doctors. No banks. No fuss.

They'd been brought up, Jim and his brothers, enjoined to be *men*: trained to avoid complaint, to endure ... and to be enormously lonely ...

The days of my return were haunted by our regret for him. That big solid man with the unfathomable shyness, given less to words than to the shrug and the grin—or stiff movements of his large mutilated hands. Dorothy remembered an exchange, when they met a friend who said Jim looked extraordinarily well. 'You've seen a fine red apple, haven't you,' said Jim, with a scorn only partly addressed at his friend, 'that when you cut into it is rotten in the middle?'

The friend had laughed. It was, after all, only old Jim putting one of his familiar shrugs into words.

On my way to Bush House, where Jenny Mallet was amused by my new African informedness, I noticed black men and women in the streets, in the underground, looking grey, bereft of the great universal brightness that justified their colour. Coloured people exiled to colourlessness. They seemed not to be standing upright.

I missed the women of Kampala, wearing those dresses, each an ocean of cloth, that were based on the dresses of Victorian missionaries' wives. The missionaries had said they must clothe their nakedness, and they'd seized on the obvious model, turning its propriety into a challenge to the senses: those bright red, yellow, blue, green frills at the waist, that proclaimed the backside, and the frilled blouse that shouted out the existence of the breasts, and those billowing leg-of-mutton sleeves ...

The weather back in Britain was hideous. I sat in my room at home rewriting the encyclopaedia of education, and the wind took the rain and threw it across the field I faced. And when I went to London the pavements swam with growing and vanishing circles of rain.

I dreamt of a newspaper item: 'In a series of raids at dawn this morning, the police rounded up the gang responsible for the recent weather.'

I tried to patch the gaping holes in my African diary. But there was too much to do simply to keep up with the present:

cascades of books to review. How could I achieve some elbow-room in my life? In any case, keeping a diary was merely another helpless attempt to stay alongside of events.

Well, as an example of life's precipitance: here was this long-haired, bony, quick-witted stranger about to go to university, who apparently was my son. We moved through life stitch by comprehensible stitch, but at any moment were startled out of our wits by the pattern it turned out to have made.

And the skirt and blouse I'd bought in the market in Kampala were simply too small for Kate. It was a blow she took kindly. I thought of the sorrowful comedy of ageing, and how that, too, came stitch by stitch. There'd been a moment when my quick Kate had become my slower Kate, and lost the shape that was youth. It was a positive moment, but I'd missed it.

I had a bad dream in which Kate, but not quite Kate, was leaving me, but not certainly me, to look after some elderly relative, who might not have been entirely elderly.

I was caught up in Englishness again. And spoke carefully to my father, on the phone, about Jim's death. Because my father was going soon into hospital for an operation for gallstones.

2

'These little black dictators ... as I call them,' he said, raising a hand to silence the protest I'd not had time to utter. 'That's my opinion. I don't want to argue about it. Little Hitlers.' His hand went up again. 'That Nkrumah. That little Kenneth Kaunda, or whatever his name is. Sweats a lot, that man. Never see him but he's sweating. One of your young fellows from television asks him a question and he starts sweating.'

'It's hot in Africa,' I exclaimed.

My father's hand flew up. 'I daresay you think you know all about it. A week here ... a week there ...'

'Thirty seconds is long enough to discover that Africa is hot,' I suggested helplessly.

'I don't want to argue! Then there's your Neary —Nairy ... whatever he calls himself. Awful names they have, all of them.'

'So they're guilty of having African names ...'

'You're getting excited.' My father smiled comfortably. 'You don't want to do that. Not at your age. Sitting down all day at the typewriter. Your heart's probably not up to much excitement ... What was I saying? Well, yes, they're all little dictators.'

'Some'—I really should smile and be silent—'are not at all little. Kenyatta—'

'Ah, Jomo!' My father was always inclined to favour a public person with an informal, or informal-sounding, first name. He'd not have been so partial to George Brown if that politician had been called ... oh, anything even mildly hoity-toity ... Christopher Brown, perhaps ... He smiled fondly. 'With his fly whisk.' He mimicked the action of a whisk. 'Makes me laugh, that man. I suppose he's a rascal, like all the rest ... but ... Pity he's black. Holds the place together. Yes ... Kenya—stands out from the others.'

'Oh good heavens,' I said.

'Of course, we don't really know what it's like.'

'Why not ask me? I've been there.'

'You've been there, but what have you seen?' my father mused, briskly. 'No, it would be interesting to know what was really going on. Not that I've any interest in it. What does it matter to me? They can dance their little war dances as much as they like, for all I care.' He laughed enormously.

'One thing you have to look hard for in Kenya,' I said, still unable to be silent. 'A war dance.'

'With their fly whisks,' said my father, dreamily.

'Oh damn it,' I said. 'Really, Dad. Of course I've only seen a bit of the surface, and a bit of what lies beneath it. But those things I *have* seen, and I do know lots of Kenyans, so why don't you ask—?'

'I think your mother would like us to join her in the

kitchen,' said my father smoothly. 'Dinner, I think. Or lunch, as I suppose you and Catherine call it.'

The friendship with the new people next door, the Butlers, hadn't lasted. Their ever being seen as tolerable neighbours had been the less likely because he, too, had been a civil servant, and she was given to pretty painting and dressing, a woman of the kind that, because his sexual interest was aroused, caused my father to speak with coarse scorn. 'Shouldn't think there's anything she doesn't powder!' Somehow they'd passed muster for a month or so, but the reaction when it came was severe. I think it was precipitated by the Butlers talking too much of their son, who was a lawyer; something, it seemed, between an articled clerk and a QC, with a strong tendency to occupy a position of vague authority in the latter area. It was harmless boasting, I guess, but it irked my father. He was reduced, mother hinted, to using me as a counter; equally vaguely referring to some obscure eminence of mine, in the general direction of a kind of broadcasting never audible in Britain.

Later, as he had done often before with so many neighbours, he set out to trap Butler into demonstrable untruths. He'd ask if Butler's son was ever in such a legal place in such and such and such a legal street, and when his neighbour said yes, he *was,* funny you mention that, *quite often* ... then my father would recall that such and such a legal place had been demolished years before, or was in quite another legal street. 'I like pricking his little bubbles,' he said. As to Mrs Butler: 'There she goes,' he'd exclaim, peering through the curtains, 'covered with lipstick up to her—'

And my mother's snuffing cry, on which he depended.

With hospital so close, he was hitting out at more than Mrs Butler. He sat by the window, consumed with frightened hostility to us all. 'There she goes!—old cow! They're Catholics! Go to confessional every morning! I don't know what they do overnight that they have to—' Kate clutched my hand. He caught the action in the angrily watchful corner of an eye. 'Ah!—we say you only do that when you've had a quarrel!' I felt Kate's fingers dig into my flesh, in mistake for her own.

101

He now had colour television. 'We wanted to see it before we died.' Hollow laughter. 'What else do we want to do before we ... pass away?'

Kate and I went walking—desperately in need of escape from that unhappy spite. Kate said he was poisoned physically, of course, and perhaps only a saint could avoid some mental poisoning.

When we returned I said the air made me sleepy. 'Oh poor little fellow!' my father cried.

3

So now it was the time for hospitals. My father, then my mother, then he again, a cruel alternation—and though in the end each made a vow not to agree to the other's being taken away—were snatched out of all ordinary context: placed, pale and threatened, in the busy ugliness of those places that ... Well, I could never understand why, since most who came to them were in a state of trembling unhappiness, they were, to begin with, so simply hideous.

My mother had been the first to be stricken, some years before. It had happened in the night: she had suddenly bled enormously, and my father had run back and forth with rags, cottonwool. He hadn't known how to bear it, with his little world bleeding to death. A doctor had come, a locum, and vaguely administered pills. The bleeding had continued. The doctor had come again and rung the hospital, and off she'd gone ...

In a curious way hospitals were to make my mother cross. They were institutions that made an offer of her greatest pleasure—a whole cast of new people, to be watched and wondered about—in the worst possible conditions: when she was too ill to give them her full attention. The worst being over, she did indulge her curiosity, peering up and down the ward from her pillow, anxious not to miss some clue as to character, some telling little gesture or remark or exchange, some mere fragment of an incident on which she could build one of her amazingly confident stories—preferably with appalling under- or overtones. My father was never more annoyed by this habit of hers of finding other people more interesting than him. It had always happened in restaurants: mother's eye on any table but the one they sat at, her ear attuned to other voices than his. At times he'd been reduced to snapping, 'What did I say? What was the last thing I said?' In hospital it was worse, because my father was going out of his way to be kindly and, as he thought, self-effacing. Unrecognisably good-natured, he would sit at mother's bedside and, faced with her wandering gaze, her tendency to interrupt some statement of his concern with an urgent, 'See that old lady over there! She's ...', would slowly lose his temper. Then it was very nearly back to the dinner tables of my childhood: my father crying, 'What do I care about ... ?'

Yet at the end of almost any hospital visit the softer man took over. Though she said he would know wickedly well what to do if she went, he was frightened that she would leave him. He would rather have her inattentive than not have her at all.

'He stood out from the others,' said my mother, describing his arrival in hospital. Poor man, this distinction—a certain crispness of pyjamas, his general handsome neatness—was not to last. But getting either of them into hospital was for my mother primarily a matter of organising the greatest possible spruceness. She was exporting examples of her skill and concern as a housewife. When we were children she'd been endlessly worried about the condition of our underwear, and the view of it that might be expressed by ambulance men, nurses, surgeons and others if we happened to be knocked down by a bus. 'Such marvellously clean underpants and vests!' these public servants would cry, looking down on our little bleeding bodies.

On this visit of ours some days after his operation, she was deeply anxious about his fate, but this was not incompatible with very great enjoyment of his absence. She was having an orgy of actually seeing people, going, by God, freely into their houses, opening the front door of the bungalow and allowing people to enter, not bothering to sleep in the afternoon. She rose at seven every morning and had instant breakfast instead of hanging around till nine, as my father had laid it down that they must. She was suddenly the little boss of her house and world, and full of stories of my father's misanthropy and her struggles against it. There'd been a recent unexpected visit—imagine that!—by a nephew and his wife, and my father, following his indignant cry of 'We're having tea!', had kept them on the doorstep. She'd had to join him in the hall and speak to him sharply. 'Ask them *in*, Dick!' And the astonished visitors, expecting open arms and finding closed ones!—and waiting for my father to think his way round his surely unchallengeable principle that callers—however closely related—who came—from however great a distance—without appointment at teatime must forfeit all hope of admission.

Having always tended to enlist inanimate objects in her army, my mother now suggested that the bungalow itself was enjoying this relaxed regime of hers. It liked having its doors opened, and thrilled to the tread of strangers.

Such childish disloyalty to my father, side by side with the most stubborn childish loyalty to him!

She withdrew into deep anxiety when the time came to visit the hospital. Her face vanished under powder, and she drew an inept mouth on it with lipstick. It was her traditional disguise for great occasions. And then—there we were, looking down on my father, from whom all the marks of spruceness had vanished. His teeth were out, his skin was suddenly very old and as white as uncooked pastry, his eyes were sunken and distant. There was a pipe in his nose, a drip-feed in his arm. In a small voice he announced that he was not likely to talk or to show much interest in us. But he turned out to be wrong about this: he did talk, very slowly but distinctly, and with a reassuring, because intensely familiar, sour humour. This was my father all right, his back against the ropes but maintaining his usual sardonic relationship with opponent, referee, the booing crowd. He counted, he said, every quarter of an hour. Breathing caused 'a sort of ripple on the cesspool' inside him. He had eaten nothing for a week, and could feel interest in nothing.

'They bring tea,' he muttered. 'I have none. They bring lunch. I have none.' He stared at my mother from a very great distance and something very slowly stirred deep inside him. 'You've put too much powder on,' he said.

My poor dapper father, consumed with self-disgust. He was condemned to disorder and gross uncleanliness by the rebellion of his own body. Nothing he could do about it, though the quality of the enfeebled awareness deep inside him was still brisk, crisp. A minute, remote fury against all untidiness.

As we left I could hardly bear the sensation of being followed by his trapped eyes ...

As the days passed, he was up and down. On the very day after our visit, down. A bronchial complication had become acute, and the curtains were drawn round his bed because of the noises he made. My mother said it seemed awful, he'd been so well when he came into hospital; and the ward sister said she was not to believe it, he was a very sick man, and couldn't have gone much further without the operation.

And then, in a day or so, a transformation. Shaven, clearly on the mend. He inveighed, in a much stronger voice, against his pillows—too hard; the cups in which tea was served—too thick; the general character of the food—unspeakable. Well, that day he'd been offered fish for lunch, and it stank, and so he refused it. And they gave him Bovril and, ugh, ice-cream. And even as he told my mother about this, he felt sickness rise in him, and she scurried for a nurse, and they put the curtains round the bed and the tube in his nose again, to prevent the sickness—and returned the drip-feed to his arm.

'Daddy's on the drip-dry again!' my mother wept on the phone that night ...

The next time I saw him, he'd become a skull only: eyes deep set and rimmed with black—such illness did black your eyes!—and the voice of someone hopelessly lost. His skin was now transparent—tissuepaper skin—and his nose sharp: as sharp as, suddenly, his false teeth were, and the high pointed bone of his brow. It was a face being split apart by bones and dentures.

First came the habitual severity addressed at my mother. She was longing to look round the ward, pick up the thread of a story here and there. What had happened to that old noisy gentleman in the end bed? 'Are you listening?' She gave him

105

her guilty attention. 'Can you hear me?' A dumb nod. Well, he wanted us to listen very closely to what he had to say. It concerned a—er—unit that had been working in the hospital on—what was the damned word?—computers. It was the computers that decided if a patient was to be saved or not. He told me to fix my gaze on a cupboard that was hanging under the ward clock. 'You'll think I'm crackers! Now, look at the lock. What is the shape of it?' 'Ah,' I said, aware of my mother's anxiety and Kate's. Better if he didn't have occasion to find me obtuse. But he provided his own answer. Letter G, eh? That was the beginning of the code. 'It tells them the food—well, the sustenance—to give us ...' The rest of the letters were to be found through an interpretation of the shapes of doorhandles, screws, bedpans, the legs of beds. 'I shall probably look back in a few weeks' time and think this was all mad,' the still brisk man inside him protested.

And later: 'This substenance ... is that right?' 'Very nearly, Dad.'

The nurses, he said, were angels. 'They draw you back from the edge of the cliff ...'

He was living in a dazed world of furious marvelling! He'd come back from the edge, in the company of hunger and drugs, and now everything was an amazement to him. Flowers especially!—smells especially!—well, the smell of a cut orange was unbelievably good! He showed his thumbnail. 'See that! I've spent half an hour gloating over a drop of water, no bigger than that!'

And to me: 'Too late?' Too late, I took him to mean, to have had this revelation of the importance of simply being alive?

Strange to think how they'd swarmed in, ignoring all the locks and chains, bursting through all his closely guarded doors—these excitements, gratitudes, stirrings of an instinct to enjoy life and embrace experience.

But, I thought, alas, it was probably too late by the length of the best part of a lifetime.

He'd also heard in his head, he said—and I remembered the detail weeks later, when he was well on his way to recovery—music, lots of music—a little tune he and I had fallen in love with together, sitting in the audience round a bandstand in Tunbridge Wells, *c.* 1930, and 'some pretty music like that—what do they call it?—opera ...'

It was the only opera my father ever spoke of—and I remembered the occasion with still startled clarity. We'd decided to take my parents to see it, early in our marriage. Not a portentous opera, certainly. *Don Pasquale.* 'I don't see why, if we're taking them out, we shouldn't find something we'd all enjoy', had been my premise. Kate and I had fetched my mother and went to join my father in town. Such excursions into high life didn't suit my mother at all. Going to London filled her, always, with wan fears. Her home and the local High Street formed her only real world. Going beyond that was an act of rashness, a venture into unreality. It took her hours to disguise herself for the outing. Drowned in her best coat, smothered by her best hat, her natural rosiness expunged with powder, she'd progress with painful absence of zest: sniffing, uncomfortable. It was obvious that on such occasions she had a clear idea of the greatest happiness possible: which was to be home again.

We took her into a teashop, and there, as she'd always done, she watched over me, leaning across absent-mindedly to straighten a knife, put a spoon within my reach, scanning my face intently for my reactions to what I ate. It was hopeless trying to involve her in conversation. She'd nod, murmur, make attempts to supply the next word for you ... always getting it wrong. I was telling her about the teacher-training college I was attending—about one of the tutors, and his noisiness—and she suddenly said: 'You need a button on your shirt.' Kate's eyes flashed, and I had to wink hurriedly at her. It was a slow business, convincing Kate that behind such a remark there was no ordinarily offensive intention. Mother always said what came into her head. Since much of her time in anyone's company was spent in a close examination of what the other was wearing, these honest ejaculations often had an appearance of intolerable rudeness in the sensitive matter of dress. 'This tutor's jackets are always split under the arms, because of the way he throws his arms about ...' I said, trying to unite the topics. Kate kicked me under the table, and I vaguely realised that my tact, as so often, was marked by ... tactlessness.

My father and my sister Betty were waiting in the foyer of

the theatre, having met and whiled away an hour together beforehand. Betty told me that, in all the black stiff glory of his office dress, this Higher Executive Officer had passed some of that time in a pin-table arcade. It had always been his love, the pin-table. Standing beside him at the seaside as a child, I'd proudly thought of myself as, so to speak, the pin-table player's mate. He'd got into conversation with an attendant, about one of the machines, Betty said, and they'd agreed, with a good workman's satisfaction in the diagnosis, that it wasn't working exactly as it should ...

So to *Don Pasquale:* the music of which—or the idea of it, if no exact memory—was to sing in my father's drugged head a quarter of a century later as he drew away from the edge of the cliff. The wine-red curtain rose and, my God, they were singing in Italian. Of course. My father drew attention to his consternation by hiding it with the politest possible obviousness. My mother watched him in these matters, as she watched me when eating. Now, with the smile of someone about to faint, she made a sort of unspoken speech: 'This isn't very nice, bringing your father along to hear something in a language he doesn't understand, and finds funny, anyway —it's Italian, isn't it?' 'Ice-a-da-creamo,' my father had always cried, hearing Italian spoken—Mussolini, on the radio, often, in the 'thirties. There was, for a moment, nothing but dismay. But then another party entered fully upon the scene. Donizetti. Vivacious music. Actually, an enchanting marriage of music with gesture, expression. Chattering quartets. Ravishing weave of melodies. After twenty minutes or so of this lovely liquid silliness, I looked sideways at the profiles of the pin-table-loving civil servant, and my unusual-experience-hating mother, and saw that both were expressing ...

Captivation was the word. My insular parents, the fact is, were on that occasion taken into musically delicious custody by a person remarkably un-English, Gaetano Donizetti ...

4

I'd been rash enough to agree to lunch on my way to the BBC
with my friend Rufus. Not that there was anything remotely
unpleasant about Rufus's company. He was a writer of novels
that had turned out, rather to his surprise, to be children's
novels. Full of startling images, witty and macabre, and
deeply concerned with the world's stains—the stain of vice
but also sometimes that of virtue, for he did not take it for
granted that being good was always less of a blot than being
bad—they had a brisk enjoyability of plot and, usually, a lad
at the centre: and this was enough to make them ... well, not
adult novels. It was awkward. Rufus, I thought, was really
addressing an audience, composed of the whole family, that,
some time ago, history had unwisely dispersed.

There were two reasons for considering it rash to meet
Rufus in London. Or rather, there was one that related to
London: another that applied whatever the venue. This
second lay in the invariable situation that Rufus would be in
despair about his current novel. Having written, say, a
hundred splendid pages, he would have been overtaken by
literary dread at its worst. His ears would be full of the
imagined voices of reviewers, sneering. 'Weak ... Ill-
constructed ... Not a patch on ...' His main terror was that
the narrative had come to a halt. Since, on the whole, as a
storyteller he was quicksilver-footed, his anxiety in this
matter, and appeals for reassurance, made me feel much as if
Nureyev had stopped in the middle of a performance of
Giselle, advanced to the front of the stage and, addressing me
by name, begged me to tell him frankly if I thought his skills
were in decline. So I would sit in a pub with Rufus, as I did
this day, reading his manuscript while he watched me,
nervously hopeful. If I smiled, or raised an eyebrow: 'What's

that!' he would cry, hoarsely ... And at the end, always, as I made the noises necessary to keep him writing, he'd ask, 'Does it move? It *does* move, does it?'

It was for Rufus's sake, but also of course for my own, since these terrors were perfectly familiar, that I'd lately proposed the formation of Authors Anonymous. On the edge of despair, a writer would ring ... this number. Perhaps, in the end, actual anonymity would be found unfitting. 'Oh, Mr Greene, you mustn't worry!—it really is *marvellous! ...*'

The rashness involved in making London a meeting-place was that Rufus would certainly take me into record shops. I adored records but could not afford to buy many. Rufus claimed that he, too, could not afford them, but *did* afford them: as if he paid for them, not with money, but with determination and courageous appetite. This did not square with the actual transactions at which I'd been present in record shops. There was no problem in watching Rufus buy records: though it could hurt, at the very simple level of jealousy and covetousness. The trouble was that he always wanted me to buy records, too. 'Aren't you going to buy anything?' he would ask, plaintively. 'I don't think I can afford ...' 'But this new recording of *Semele*—you simply must have it.' 'Lovely idea, Rufus—but ...' 'Oh dear,' Rufus would say, expressing his habitual deep disappointment in me.

Disappointing Rufus was *not* a pleasure. However, on this occasion his interest was focussed on loudspeakers. He was afflicted with one of his inflammations in respect of these, which occurred at regular intervals. The loudspeakers he had, and that for at least three months had boomed away around him as he worked, highly regarded, had earned his sudden scorn. I stood by and made amazed noises while, amid an ecstasy of nervous inquiries, he bought replacements that would not have been sniffed at by the BBC.

Where I found myself in the studio with a novelist from Ghana who'd brought his little daughter with him. I was interviewing the novelist, but found myself with duties in respect of his daughter, too. With her black head cracked with partings, and the horns of wound-up hair that made it also like a black grocer's bag twirled at the corners, she elected to settle in my lap. I was therefore at one and the same time an experienced broadcaster and a far less experienced provider of seating for a small child whose African eyes, as we made our recording, were in and out of hiding ...

Jenny Mallet had stories for me, from the school in Kenya where I'd asked for writing set in that brilliant valley rather than detective stories set nowhere. There were interesting domestic tales: of the luck of finding a school place; of tragedy hingeing on the death of cattle; of going into Nairobi and being amazed by a city that must be the very hub of the world. Here and there were references to the extraordinary redness of the soil and the prevalence of poinsettias that reflected what I'd said rather than what they felt. But I was pleased to have turned some literary noses in another direction ...

I showed Jenny an article I'd been writing about my involvement with African literature. In it I'd tried to express my impatience with groups of my fellow-countrymen. 'With some critics, for example,' I'd written, 'who discuss African writing with what seems to me an abysmal absence of proper excitement or informed sympathy. With many readers, who do not miss the latest American, British or French novel, but seem content to read little if any African writing. With teachers, who fail to note that a new great literature has appeared on the scene, that it is grappling with problems that we all need to be aware of, even when they seem most domestically African; that it is also dealing, much of it, with a conflict of cultures and outlooks that goes to the roots of the human condition; that it is in the exciting state of a literature where all the judgements are yet to be made; that that part of it that is written in English exhibits the English language in new forms, being made to respond to new needs. I grow impatient because I have no doubt that nothing more important has happened recently in the universe of literature than this marvellous emergence of new voices in Africa. So far again as African writing in English is concerned, an important feature of that writing is that it is developing under the shadow of an already established old literature in the same language; to me, the way it has already grown away from that shadow, has so early established its own remarkable independence, is heroic, and because I admire immensely the achievements of those African writers who already have

111

given to English an African tone and resonance, I am impatient with those who fail to notice that all this is happening. It is, I know, unfair of me, in many respects, to have such strong feelings of impatience. Might I not have remained as ignorant myself but for the accident of that suggestion, ten years ago, by a BBC producer? Often I talk about African writing to literary groups, or groups of teachers, and when I express this impatience of mine, my listeners always appear duly contrite, and some say, as a group of teachers said to me very recently: "But we didn't know about it." And I recognise that it might be very easy for a British reader, even an avid reader, somehow never to meet an African novel, or simply to be timid or diffident about approaching an unfamiliar body of work. However, here I am, the outsider who has had the privilege of feeling at times at least half an insider; and it is really from thinking of myself in this way, as a non-African who feels close to his African colleagues, from time to time, that I have begun to work towards the general feeling about African writing that I have tried to embody in my very ordinary title.'

'Yes, love,' said Jenny, turning back to the first page. 'But what is this very ordinary title? It doesn't seem to be here.'

'Oh Lord,' I said. 'Well, I thought of calling it: "African Writing in English—a New World Literature." '

'Pithy,' said Jenny. 'You know what Tolstoy was originally going to call "War and Peace"?'

'No.'

'He thought it would make its way into the world quite happily,' Jenny lied, 'as "Some Reflections on the Military and Non-Military Elements in the Historical Process." '

'*Fool*,' I said …

But Richard, another producer who sought Jenny out when he was in despair—which was not seldom—overbid both her and me in this matter of naming people as fools. He thought the two of us formed a corporate fool, for taking so much so seriously. His was a curious professionalism—resting on the view that the people out of whom he made programmes were, on the whole, dreadful nonentities. They had established this by the very fact of their being programme material. It was a strange effect of working, everlastingly, to wring newsy stories and newsy issues out of

112

people, their behaviour, their activities. All the years of his working life a procession of eager people had been turned coolly into programmes by Richard: and he'd concluded that everyone was much the same, in the end—as unimportant as they were self-important, boring.

He even held that most people's names were absurd, and that they ought to be ashamed of them. And African writers were conspicuous among those who made no effort at all to replace preposterous names with sensible ones.

Though, when it came to the point, I believe, Richard didn't really think that anyone had a sensible name.

5

I escaped from the bewilderment of the encyclopaedia of education to Cornwall. Years before, when our sons were small, we'd found this cottage, a simple guest-house, set in a vast bosom of fields, with a back garden that ran down to a wood that itself ran down to the haven. You could have stepped, you thought, straight onto the silvery roof of trees as onto a floor. A lane fell one way to the haven, lifted in the other direction to a sunken silver farm and the approach to a beach that would, the tide being out, have held the entire population of Cornwall, but never did, one reason being that the way to it was a panting goatpath, itself the last descent in a sequence of them, the best of all being a path that hurried down under a fearfully torn face of cliff. Whole cities of rock were everywhere on the verge of falling. Beyond, north and south, there was more sea than was strictly possible.

Running down to the beach, by those enormous slopes— bitten grass, shale, and the final slither—I'd stand on it and breathe London out and Cornwall in. And then go and measure what the seas had done since my last visit by way of rearranging the rocks. How crazed these decorous waters must be in winter, to hurl things so huge into confusions always new.

I had a fellow guest—a bishop's widow, said Milly, who ran the guest-house. Oh, and her companion. Too late Milly had learned that the lady had been elsewhere in the village, and they'd all said they'd not have her again. Stuck up.

It seemed too mild a judgement. All guests ate together, at Milly's, and when the bishop's widow was ushered in, her mousy companion in tow, she caught my eye and laughed. 'Well, honestly,' she said. Her amusement was plainly related to the vulgar surprise of discovering that she and her companion were not dining alone. I, she said over the soup, was clearly learned—a philosopher, perhaps? I wrote theses in Greek? ... I imagined my father exposed to such affectations. But perhaps he would have admired the old lady for refusing so absurdly to be common? Many old ladies in our own family, certainly, had spent their lives being obsequious companions to just such old ladies as this—who were spoken of most respectfully. (Dear Lady Taylor!) She expressed genteel incredulity ... no, mocking *grande dame* incredulity ... at the fare: being especially amazed by Milly's pease pudding. ('What *is* that curious dish?') She'd never intended to stay here, but there was nowhere else. She'd have given her companion her usual holiday in the south (for this was not *her* holiday, at all), but there was oil on the beaches. She'd passed this cottage in the summer and, dear me, it was *full* of people, and *children*. Wouldn't dream of staying here at the height of the season. The room she was in would take *four*—crammed in like sardines they must be.

It dawned on her, from some absence of distance between Milly and me, that I was no stranger to the cottage. 'I think you're rather *it*, here!' She commissioned me to do some 'detective work'—'I'm sure you don't look as though you'd mind.' They wanted to be up at seven in the morning—could I make *discreet inquiries* and discover if this was all right with *her*? 'I feel frightened, for the first time in my life.' Well, Milly had frowned once or twice, seeing some of her more famous items of food reacted to with cries of amazement and disbelief.

And so I became a go-between, relating the indignantly amused kitchen to the incredulously tittering sitting-room.

114

She was a flatterer. I came there, I said, usually with my wife.—Wife! I was *married!*—Well, yes.—Family? Surely not?—Two boys.—How old?—Eighteen and fifteen.—No! *No!* Quite *impossible!* I looked no more than eighteen myself! —And when I said doubtfully that they might scramble down to the beach, but then must walk with care on the rocks, she said I could have no need to take care anywhere— must be *like a young goat!*

I couldn't conceive of anything more respectable than a bishop's widow, yet felt myself at times quite unrespectably appraised. I imagined a story about the wicked career of the relict of a decent churchman. By Zola. *The Bishop's Widow.*

Everybody she spoke of was a creature. This woman was a charming creature. This man was a horrid creature. One or two people were nobodies.

I lay, reading then sleeping, on the cliff day after day, waking to a glittering scene framed with mist; or one afternoon, to a spectacle of headlands and horizon smothered under a deep blue haze, the sun going behind a cloud and making a tent of rays that grew wider and wider, each pole of the tent standing in a pool of light on the otherwise blurred blue of the sea.

It was exotic, exotic. How did *this* exotic differ, as it certainly did, from the exotic of East Africa, still so vivid to me? And how would it differ from that of West Africa, where it seemed I might go next year some time, so that what I now felt as a literary difference between those two poles of the continent might become a difference between two remembered realities? ...

The beach was bared and smothered, bared and smothered. On the silver tangle of treetops in the wood was now laid a rough gold. Sheep in the fields and flocks of clouds cropping a blown blue sky.

And everywhere the distant old green hat of the bishop's widow, and the grey pursuing hat of her companion ...

Kate joined me, and then, happy with all that air and Milly's kindness, we made for New Chilton. Going from *there* to *there* was especially difficult—from friendliness to the prospect of its reverse.

How pleasant, we thought as so often before, if we were received with smiles; if there were tea in the garden, and jokes. The extent to which this was *not* how we were received appalled us. My father was at his grimmest: his voice clipped and cold. He launched within minutes of our arrival into a long attack on dogs, for fouling the footpaths, and seagulls, for fouling his roof. Dogs, he implied, were owned for the specific reason that they *were* footpath-foulers. To put it plainly, it was for this very aspect of their activity that they were purchased in the first place by their owners, largely disgusting old ladies and obscene old men. The dogs were taken out of a morning and again of an evening, as in some malign military operation, precisely with the aim of fouling the footpaths of New Chilton. 'I don't want shit on my shoes every time I go out,' snapped my father, as if dog-owners might have been working on the theory of his having positively the opposite desire. As to seagulls, it was the familiar complaint; they simply homed in on the bungalow with immense needs in respect of excretion and the express intention of satisfying those needs whilst flying over my father's roof. No suggestions were offered as to how, given that New Chilton was so very much on the sea, and seagulls were so very much seabirds, the situation might be altered. My father was simply enraged by the existence of seagulls and by his notion of the inconsiderate coarseness of their habits. 'I'd like to shoot the lot of them,' he barked.

'Dick!' said my mother, meaning: Ted and Kate are here, and we should talk about quite nice things, quite nicely. 'Why the devil should I get dogshit on my shoes and birdshit on my roof!' he rapped. 'Oh Dick!' Then his inflamed condition began to detach itself from dogs and seagulls, obviously almost random fuel. The real cause of his anger appeared. Did I know, he asked, leaning sore-eyed across the table—on which my mother had just placed the sponge cake on which she'd lovingly laboured in our honour—that during the First World War he'd brought a girl to his brother George's place, asking for accommodation for the night, and that George had refused accommodation, except that which would have obliged my father and the girl to sleep together? And that later the girl had a child and made a claim of paternity against my father, and that his brother George refused to give evidence in his favour attesting that that immoral offer of his had been declined. And so a paternity

116

order had been made. 'I know you've heard the story from George,' he barked. 'Oh no I haven't,' I said. And indeed I hadn't. My only informant in the matter had been my mother who, long ago, had told me about my half-brother, for she was sure the child was my father's; and how paying the weekly amount exacted under the paternity order had made life even more difficult for them; and how, once, long after the order had lapsed, the boy had written to my father, asking to see him, and my father had torn the letter up, in frightened fury, crying, 'He's got no claim on me!' 'Let me just say,' I said, struggling to keep my temper, 'that I've not heard this from George.' 'I know damned well you have,' he shouted. 'Don't tell me you haven't!'

And then a lifetime of patience snapped. 'Kate,' I cried. 'Let's go home. I can't take any more of this. Oh, I *can't* take any more of this!' My hands were dancing in front of my eyes as they used to do in adolescent furies. All this raking up of old malice! It had been so horribly the background of my childhood, so that I'd thought for a long time that a family was an organisation designed for hostilities. I was in the grip of an enormous rage. When the blur of it had passed, and I could see again, I observed that Kate and my mother were in tears, and my father had vanished. Mother, out of her tears, was making a characteristically miscellaneous set of statements, covering the wide range of contradictions with which she had to live. 'Why does he have to do such things?' she cried. Then: 'He's my husband, and I still love him.' Then: 'His heart is bad—I'll have to nurse him.' And finally: 'No one knows the cruel things I have to put up with.' It struck me wildly that I'd been present at a ceremony at which my father was honoured, caressed, arrested and cursed in a single sweeping celebration.

I stroked her hair and went in search of him. He was in the kitchen, staring out of the window. I put my arm round his shoulder and told him how complicatedly angry he'd made me. He'd implied that I was a liar, and that Kate and I listened complacently to bad stories about him; and he'd wounded me more than anything by believing that I'd think ill of him for having undergone such a common misfortune. He said then, quietly, that he'd thought only that I'd heard one side of the story from others. He wanted me to know he'd paid for sixteen years for something he didn't do. 'I shall soon be going to Heaven,' he murmured, 'and I wanted you to know the truth.'

Oh, the terrible frightened irony of that phrase 'going to Heaven'! It stood for who knew what belief of my father's in respect of his fate after death. When I'd recently shown him a photograph I'd taken of him, laughing, a pallid guffawing skull—'Now I know what I shall look like in my box!' he'd said. Death was a dreadful terror to him, worse for that ridiculous imagery of heavens, and coffins.

I felt a terrible pity, then, for the torment he inflicted upon himself. Who needed hell, with such long premonitions of hell to play with?

The shock remained: of having, under whatever provocation, quarrelled bitterly with an old man with a weak heart. As he grew more in need of my patience, so my patience seemed to weaken. I was deeply glad of Kate's approval. 'I should have been ashamed of you,' she said, adding to all these unexpectednesses, 'if you hadn't lost your temper!' The switch in tone was total; we chattered brightly, we were most improbably in agreement about everything. My father, to clinch whatever terrifying truce we'd blundered into, took me round the garden; and had respect for my ignorant murmurings as if I'd been that great television gardener for whom he had such enormous admiration, and whose name I was constantly forgetting.

I found myself thinking of that failure of Uncle George's to corroborate my father's story. If that had been what really happened. There had never been any way of checking the accuracy of any assertion made by any member of the family. I realised how much of my childhood had been coloured by this curious attitude to truth of whatever kind. It was less that my family were liars than that they took a special, disparaging view of the very idea of accuracy. They always seemed to be arguing about *versions* of events rather than about what actually happened. The conflict was not between truth and falsehood but between lie and lie.

Well, how difficult for any human being to walk the straight line of the truth for more than a few seconds at a time! I knew from my habit of keeping a diary that much more often than not the checking of memory against recorded fact proved memory to be wrong; usually, not mildly so, but wrong in some quite recklessly inventive fashion. It was wrong about the number, and identity, of the people present; about the setting; about the date; about the cause for a happening, and its consequences. Memory inflated, conflated, deflated, was an immoderate maker of fiction.

A division among human beings, however: between those who were committed to at least some small attempt to establish accuracy, and those with no such commitment? In my family, I saw, the commitment had always been minimal. They had not expected to be truthful, or to hear much that was true ...

Was that right? Or had they never measured the degree to which they were products, and producers, of fantasy?

6

I took him to a pub, and was given a long sad glimpse of his official career.

'I worked,' he said, 'damned hard—for years I thought of nothing else—neglected my home ... And now I wish I hadn't.' He looked every day at the obituary column in the *Telegraph* in the hope of seeing a report of the death of his superior, Tom Elam.

Curious! He was very capable of relishing the death of those he particularly disliked. I'd read out, startled, on one visit, the news of Epstein's death. 'Time that man died!' my father had commented.

Tom Elam! Never was a fond form of a man's Christian name used less fondly. I had no idea how he qualified as a target of my father's special hatred, but imagined he was someone thought of as being socially at ease—much made of his living in Surrey, apparently a sure mark of

119

arrogance and conceit—and given to doing quickly things that took my father time. After all, my father—drawing on what he remembered of an extremely brief education—had crept into the Civil Service as an old soldier, in 1920. He whose habit it was to throw things away—there'd have been no museums or libraries or collections of anything whatever if he'd been in charge of human affairs—never destroyed a London County Council Labour Certificate of TOTAL Exemption from Attendance at School that was issued in respect of him on 9 June 1906, and affirmed that this Exemption was within the usual conditions: that is, that he was not less than twelve years of age (he was three months over thirteen) and had been certified by one of His Majesty's Inspectors of Schools as having reached the Seventh Standard. Amid this plethora of capital letters it was indicated, in smaller print, that since he was indeed an elderly person of thirteen plus, he might freely be employed in a Factory or Workshop. The reason for this Exemption, not noted on the certificate, was that his widowed mother needed his help to keep her and sundry younger brothers.

Tom Elam, on the other hand, had almost certainly walked into the Civil Service, unambiguously qualified.

'A lifetime of public service,' my father said now, in the New Chilton pub. 'I suppose that's all right, though no one's interested.'

'That's all right': so often his euphemism for 'That's all, appallingly, wrong!' He had this feeling, which you might expect in someone who'd narrowly missed being Prime Minister, that the nation had been ungrateful. But when it came to the point, not so much the nation (though he didn't easily admit to a narrowing of the number of culprits) as, for example, his former colleagues—and his son. Oh, I'd certainly been ungrateful, lacked interest! I'd been one of those who yawned in the face of my father's public-spirited record. As a school-leaver, I'd refused to accept the fate long intended for me—that of joining the Civil Service and avenging him for the indignities he'd suffered. He had wanted me, I think, positively to displace Tom Elam, had imagined a scene in which I entered Tom Elam's office and, perhaps with a certain amount of practical violence, ejected him.

I'd always been aware that my father's life at work was as

warlike as his life at home. When he discussed it with my mother, it was always in terms of his unpopularity. And of his pride in being unpopular: since the reason for it, he implied, was that he was a strict man, who believed (against, it seemed, some general contrary current of belief) that his underlings should work the full day for which they were paid, from the first to the last stipulated moment. It didn't, he recognised, make him very amiable. 'They think I'm a bugger! Well, so do I! If insisting on a good day's work is being a bugger, then I'm a bugger!'

The trouble was, I guess, that he was a bugger who caused pain and sometimes despair. One of my mother's most famous refusals to accept his behaviour occurred when he'd come home with stories of his treatment of an inefficient clerk. The man, it was clear, had reasons for being unhappy —his family had broken up, he'd begun to drink. In my father's running account of his attempts to bring this unfortunate man to order, the episode that made my mother openly angry was one in which the man broke down and wept bitterly under a more than usually cruel reproof. My father told the story as yet another example of his disinterested probity. 'Lots of people have troubles, but they've got to leave them behind when they come to work. We'd never get anything done if we all blubbered all day long. Do they think I've got nothing to cry about? But I put it all behind me when I get to the office.' Mother said, 'That was a very wicked thing to do, Dick!'

And he was uneasy, miserably uneasy. When it came to it, she always had the power to make him feel he'd acted badly. It was rarely, alas, the power to make him act well. He hadn't really the gift for that.

7

But what came on him twice before the end was a sudden dazed beneficence—like his experience in hospital, a glimpse of that amiable way of living for which he had no consistent knack. The pleasure of being agreeable always took him by surprise, as if it had been a matter of some quite novel pioneering extension of the human spirit. He always meant to sustain it: he never did.

The first occasion came now: simply his golden wedding.

The mere prospect of it made him enormously benign. Various grand settings were canvassed, and he smiled upon them all. We decided on a splendid hotel; he said yes, and of course we must have a room of our own, and he would try to recall what a colleague long ago had told him about the merits of different sorts of champagne. No clouds, no shadows, must hang over this day. It was with untypical caution that he referred to the only possible blot, which lay in our son Tom's hair. Tom's hair was very long and henna'd. He was not at all an undergraduate as my father had expected an undergraduate to be. He was also given to wearing old flannel shirts without the collars. My father's life had largely been spent struggling to put behind him a world of men with collarless flannel shirts. He didn't imagine that Tom would turn up for the golden wedding in such a shirt—or in the mildewed top hat he'd worn on a recent suburban walk with Kate and me: but he feared he might appear capped with a tangle of red hair. To my father such a coiffure was characteristic of … gypsies. Had he struggled to keep abreast of Tom Elam only to have a gypsy as a grandson?

'We feel,' he wrote, 'that the hotel might refuse to admit Thomas if he appears with his hair unshorn. I am afraid, in fact, that if he intends to come looking as he does at the moment, we must ask him not to come at all. This would be a very great sorrow to his grandmother.'

Using the complicated channels necessary at the time, I passed on this demand to Tom, who used channels equally complicated to inform me in return that there was no cause for anxiety. Taking the steps required to fit into the general setting of this golden wedding would not count as an abandonment of important revolutionary positions, I could calm the old people ...

And the day came: a full summer's day. My father was in a sweet state of nerves. He thought of me as his lieutenant, and treated me as one. It was a golden day for me, too, being so treated. I was 'Ted' from morning to night. 'I daresay they'll ask you what you want to drink, when you arrive. See that everybody gets what they need.' And I must make everyone choose what he wanted to eat. They'd bring round the menus. That's how it was usually done. He relied on me to see that everyone chose exactly what he wished.

Tom arrived, his hair beautifully abbreviated, the trimmings in a bag, which, with explanations, he presented to my mother. 'Oh Tom!' she cried, not able to take in anything that anyone said on any topic at all. It was days later when she opened the bag and discovered the odd nature of the gift.

A blue day: three polished hire cars; this beautifully attentive hotel. There were armchairs by the French windows; a round dining table; waiters who delighted my father by being Italian. His usual view of things Italian, revolving round a sarcastic assessment of the language, was absolutely in abeyance. But then his usual view of almost everything was in abeyance ...

He fussed immensely over menus and wine lists; and my mother, always capable however dazed of drawing shrewdly on her stack of memories, told me he'd embarrassed her once at a hotel they'd visited during a coach tour of the Highlands. He'd loudly reproached a waiter for removing the knives and forks they were not going to use: 'I resent your doing this, you know—I'm not going to put them in my pocket!'

And lunch, at that round table! Our younger son, Dan, his tongue loosened by wine, lending his ear (which had to be guessed at) to my sister, who was tipsily grave; it was some

123

unlikely conference at *Alice in Wonderland* level, a pleasant young Knave and a Queen of some colour or other, heightened.

And my father anxiously happy, tolerating even the misbehaviour of unsuccessful new false teeth. My mother worried—about him and what he drank, and the effect on his stomach, and about herself and what she ate, and the effect on *her* stomach. For these pleasures they might pay with groaning nights ... even with return visits to those dreadful, dreaded hospitals ...

Hers was the day's shortest speech. 'I'm glad,' she said, as glasses prepared to be tipsily lifted, 'I married the man I loved.'

8

But it was Dorothy, Kate's mother, who went into hospital now—to die.

She'd gone bewildered through the year since Jim's death, and suddenly, one day, couldn't walk. A leg blackened. For the last time she left the house with the cactuses and the frail doors and came to us.

'I don't want to go in the spring,' she said piteously, as if claiming a right to choose. The pear tree in the garden, visible from where she lay, was only too obviously shouting its head off with blossom, and preparation for summer. A few days before a bundle of old sticks, the entire garden was now a foam and rage of flower. It was coming, and she was going. I shrank a little as I entered the room where she lay, not knowing how to respond to the look in her eyes of fierce accusing despair. She was angry, she was raw with anger, an eighty-year-old woman appalled by the continuing world, by her unthreatened children, by the assertiveness of new blossom that had always been more important to her than people. Spring itself was a dagger sunk into her heart. I felt her anger wherever I went in the house, and the accusation she was levelling at us all, of not being able to care enough that she was dying. There should have been some step we could take on her behalf, some protest or demonstration: we should have been busy with challenges to death itself. We should have been writing letters, at least. Oh, Dorothy's lifelong belief in the importance of writing letters: to the council, the water board, your child's school ... Instead, our apologetic eyes, our unconvincing smiles. We felt seared by her essential contempt for all that ...

And the ambulance came along the lane, and went away again, with her in it, abandoned to the last chapter, the hospital ... where we found her, her anger become a blackness and congestion that had already killed her feet, was killing her legs: a cruelly slow failure of the basic system, of the flow of blood. She stared at us, looking now like someone who'd been beaten up—not just her eye but her whole face blacked. And the last day came, with a call from the hospital; it might be as well for Kate and me to come ... Now she'd been monstrously ill-treated by the process of dying; it had turned her into a single great black bruise. It was a Saturday afternoon. Death gave her moments of understanding, moments of puzzlement. Her dying mind ran backwards and forwards across the years. She urged Kate to cut sandwiches for tea. Fifty years adrift, she rode in an early car, at Jim's side. Then clarity again: she wanted to know where her grandchildren were, this very day, displaying meticulous knowledge of their possible whereabouts. Kate and I sat side by side; a neighbour and another came, were helplessly gentle and incredulous, vanished. It became simply a long after-noon, turning into a long evening ...

There was, in the hospital, a kind of ordinariness about that evening that seemed very odd indeed, since it was, for her, such an extraordinary one. We took it in turns to hold her swollen and discoloured hand. The skin was slack, without lustre. She was growing cold, though she claimed she was not. 'I wish I weren't so tired,' she said—as if this was not quite what she wanted to say: as if these were the only words for the vital draining away of herself that was occurring. There were fragments, perhaps of food, in her mouth, and

125

now and then her hand would come up, clawed, groping, to fumble for them. It was all dry—mouth, hand. 'All the moisture,' she said, 'has gone from my body.' I grinned at her, and the huge eyes stared until, very slowly, her mouth, fallen sideways, shaped an answering grin. 'Your hair is turning grey,' she said, with a sudden little vigour. 'I hadn't noticed before.' 'So is yours,' I said. She didn't smile. 'Well, I'm old.'

It was, half hour by half hour, a fading and distancing, as if the front room of her existence was being vacated. From somewhere much further back came a sudden agitation: 'Will someone sign my pension form? The Post Office will be closed tomorrow.' In all that growing blankness, something hung on to the knowledge that it was Saturday. She wanted tea, and it was brought, in a special cup with a spout, and she was able to let a little of this, the last of all the cups of tea she'd had in eighty years, bubble into her mouth.

She wanted to know where Kate was—again and again. Then some impulse of panic started up in the dying body: 'Oh, I'm so lazy. I must get up, I must get up.' 'You shall get up soon, dear.' But the desperation died in her eyes as soon as it came. Responses were now fewer and fewer. The nightly business of the ward took place—the bringing and taking away of bedpans, the giving of medicines. An orderly, gently polite, brought us armchairs: said he would take us in turns to the visitors' room, to rest, if we wished. The lights were turned out, and a special soft light provided for us.

I went out twice into the bustling air to phone Dan, who tried hard—I felt the effort he made—to be sad for his grandmother, for us; but he had his girl with him, could not keep the sound of bright young Saturday night out of his voice. A nurse brought us tea and biscuits. Kate had cried, but was not crying now. It was a kind of awe we felt—a species of perfectly practical awe. It was all part of the matter-of-fact machinery of existence, and the awe was matter-of-fact, too.

An old lady in the bed opposite farted in her sleep. The ward sighed, uttered little fading cries of despair.

For a long time there was nothing but the quickening and shortening of breath. It seemed an increasingly urgent task, dying, but secret, a business now very deep in the body on the bed.

126

We walked in the grounds while she was washed, and returned to find that breath now came very short. Her thin white hair, which she'd wanted to have cut, lay scattered on the pillow, but Kate smoothed it into a shape, and she looked for a moment quite like a young girl. But the face became more and more distorted, the mouth fell sharply sideways, the head slipped from the pillow. The eyes stared hugely, but seemed to see nothing. A nurse came and put her head in an easier position. 'All right now, Mrs Brown?' It was a brisk mechanical habit of showing care, of being kindly, even when it was a matter of addressing something almost dead, no longer having a name ...

Now the breathing became very noisy, there seemed even a kind of rowdiness about it, and there were little whimperings. The nurse came again and, this time, looked at the clock, made a note. I touched Kate's arm, for it was clearly the end. The last strugglings of breath were immensely laboured, and all the final debris, air and mucus, rattled in the throat. The whole body stirred—and there was one last, long, loud whimper of panic. I thought it was the most unconscious crying of nerves and brain as their last defences fell, and death made ready to dash in. Kate was very much shocked by it, and talked afterwards of her mother as 'a wounded animal', but the cry seemed to me as mindless as a baby's cry at birth. A protest and gasp from a dying machine from which all real personality, capable of suffering in any conscious sense, had surely vanished ... Surely?

The very last loud puffings of breath came from the mouth only, and suddenly—one couldn't quite see how one knew this—the body that had been able to quiver, to stir, however minutely, had become absolutely incapable of movement; death had happened. But even as tears flowed from Kate's eyes, and death was already completely present, the mouth was forced slightly open by a few last little bubbles of air.

And I thought, as we made our shocked and astonished way home, that I'd never seen anything more beautiful. It had been like nothing so much as an oil lamp going out—the flame shortening and guttering and becoming noisy, as the last licks of oil were drawn up. And I saw very well how it was that people spoke of the spirit departing. There had been the most absolute sense of going that I had ever known ...

127

So that's how it was! That was how life took its leave!

And all those eighty years dispelled, dispersed and cancelled. Like drawing a roll of film out of a camera and letting the light suddenly, in no time at all, destroy all the images it carried, all that evidence that time had ever existed ...

The little, temporary life surrounding the bone, I thought for days afterwards, glimpsing Kate's face, my own in a mirror. And the oddest thing about the dead—I'd always felt it, reading history, biography, collected letters—was that they'd entertained the idea that they were alive.

There was an awful sense of being some sort of burglar, of burglary being made enormously easy, when we went through the house clearing it of Dorothy and Jim. The occupants of the house had surrendered, in respect of its security, most remarkably. They'd left it wide open to us, their burglarious survivors. Kate and I went through it with the distaste and unease induced by such a role. Here, so absolutely at our mercy, were Jim's secrets, Dorothy's privacies. And yet, when it came to it, how little there was for which either word was apt.

Not anywhere even one slightly rash scrap of paper.

9

It had necessarily been of interest to me—the ease, and the difficulty, of truancy when you were a freelance working at home. The ease was obvious, seeing that work and idleness were not more than a few feet apart. The difficulty was less explicable. I never wholly understood what kept me working. Perhaps it was the quality that was attributed to boys I'd taught by colleagues who didn't know how else to explain their simply remaining on the premises. Persistence. I was persistent.

I was also, most of the time, in a tangle. To proposals that I review, edit, broadcast, lecture, I'd say Yes. Then I'd add all the Yeses together and they constituted a bigger Yes than I could accommodate. Move in any direction and I tangled with a forgotten commitment. Once again, I'd overdone it.

The freelance's deepest fear, of course, was of saying No. Say No and suddenly everybody would go away, having whispered among themselves that you were someone who conceitedly cold-shouldered kindly offers of employment. Utter a single No and you were back in the hut in the forest, without a bite to eat and surrounded by the howling hunger of your children ...

An actual child of mine, my son Tom, held around this time, with a sort of tender mercilessness, that in not being back in the hut I was demonstrating that I was in the grip of complacency and materialism. This seemed to me extremely likely. Once you had taken against the idea of being hungry, it was extraordinarily difficult to know where to stop. I was definitely not uncomfortable. And it seemed vaguely to make it worse that much of what I did caused me considerable pleasure—my African programme more almost than anything else.

I was in the grip not only of materialism but also of idealism. Whichever way I turned, I felt Tom's stern eye on me ...

Much of what we did in the studio now consisted of reviews of new books, interviews with visiting authors. Africa was changing very fast. 'By the time you've taken a position on what you want to do,' Chinua Achebe told me, 'you suddenly discover that that thing is no longer important.' And he spoke of the complicated call upon his energies that caused him to shrink away from the experience that, given another world, another time, would have been for him the best of all experiences. How long did a novel take him? 'Average eight months, I think,' said Achebe, 'and it's a hell of a long time to be in prison.' The Sudanese novelist, Tayeb Salih, said he was driven by those calls and pressures to contradict the tradition of his people. It was certainly no characteristic of Arabic literature to produce short books like his. 'But I snatch moments here and there and I bring a story to a conclusion perhaps earlier than it should be.'

But the basic work of the programme remained: to give counsel to beginners. Teaching, I was being taught. I found myself advising my listeners to put their work away—and then surprise themselves with it. 'Come to it not as someone who's hot and tired with the effort of writing, but as a cool half-stranger.' Do so much with it, and no more. 'It's rather like winding a watch—you know that if you go on too long you'll break the spring, but you develop an instinct for the moment when you've wound it completely and one more turn would do damage. If you have the habit of regularly winding up your writing, as it were, you'll acquire the same sort of instinct, knowing that to do more would only harm it.' Or I'd find myself talking about the splendid mystery of the way you join bits of language to other bits of language. 'You know when someone's trying to join wood together, to make something out of wood, and he hasn't yet learned how to do joints properly—he tries nailing, and because one nail doesn't hold he tries another: and so the joint is a sort of clumsy mess of nails ... And actually, the joints don't have to be made like this. When the story flows, when the style flows, it has its own inbuilt secret joints and understood connections.'

And I was greatly moved by the belief, reflected in much of the writing, that one ought to be grand. Because it was true, of course. It is right to be grand, as against consenting to be mean, small, dull. But grandeur of language was sometimes, when sought in a language not intimately familiar, very strange to contemplate. 'There was abundant provision for partnership in the category of the gentry' was an extraordinary way of saying that he had a large choice of brides from among the well-to-do.

And as for the moment when the heroine 'moved in pandiculation toward the living room.' 'I had to look in a dictionary to find that this meant that Dillo moved with an "extension of the legs, a raising and stretching of the arms, and a throwing back of the head and the trunk, accompanied by yawning, as occurring before and after sleeping, in hysteria, etc." And I must say this gave me such a worried impression of Dillo that I wished I'd left the word alone.'

'I'm surprised they can talk, sometimes,' said my father. 'But I'll take your word for it. They can write as well.' He

130

collected laughs from the corners of the room, but none came. Kate sat biting her tongue; my mother was deaf, but wouldn't have laughed if she'd heard him.

But then—in the cupboard under the bureau in the hall, where his stock of books was accommodated, there was *King Edward's Realm,* presented to my father, as to all other London school children of the time, as a souvenir of the coronation of Edward VII on 26 June 1902. (In fact, as a label on the fly leaf confesses: 'Owing to the serious illness of the King, a public announcement was made on the 24th of June that the Coronation was postponed.') Fastened by a black safety pin to the same leaf is a red fabric label marked M, which would have admitted my father to the cheering ranks of children, had the ceremony then occurred. The book is the work of the Rev. C. S. Dawe, author of *Queen Victoria and her People,* &c.

I am not in the least confident that my father ever read this book. But its sentiments are certainly the characteristic sentiments among which—with the full approval of the Borough of Paddington, their Children's Coronation Fete Committee, the Educational Supply Association, the Church of England (of which the Rev. Dawe was a luminary) and the London County Council—my father grew up. And reading *King Edward's Realm* now—it was one of the few books in the house when I was a child, and many of its phrases are startlingly familiar to me—I am struck by a number of the attitudes it adopts. Two in particular. 'In colonising Australia little account had to be taken of the natives, who were both few and feeble.' And, in respect of the work of a pioneer force sent to search for minerals in Lobengula's territory, in Rhodesia: 'Before two years had passed it became quite clear that the Matabele warriors must be crushed before any progress can be made. *Thanks to our machine-guns and modern rifles, this was soon effected.'*

The italics are mine and not the Rev. C. S. Dawe's. He saw no reason to emphasise such a commonplace sentence.

10

And my mother ringing. He'd had a bad night, unable to breathe: they couldn't find a hospital bed for him, it having been a particularly dangerous winter for old people, but they were sending along an oxygen tent.

We woke next morning to sensational snow: a foot of it, and more where it had drifted. The shrubs in the garden were unkempt, dragged low with the weight of it; milk bottles standing outside the door were snowy nipples above the surface. There was no newspaper, no post. I tried to ring my mother, but everything was out of order. The world had come to a stop.

Then Dr Mackenzie rang. My father had pneumonia—my mother hadn't been told this was what it was—and he'd been taken urgently to hospital. He was very ill, and there would be a great strain on his heart that might well finish him. I should go at once.

So I set out in a world that made any notion of travel seem ridiculous. An hour in the local waiting room; a creeping journey to London; a snail's crawl across London; and the slowest possible train to the coast. In the urgency of it, I had brought nothing with me to eat; the train had no food to offer. We crept southwards, appalled by every snow-drift.

And there he was ... in the first bed in the ward, the bed for the most ill, eyes closed, gasping—and astonished to see me. Speaking with difficulty, he said he was sure he wouldn't come home this time. This was it. Some doctor, not his discreet Mackenzie, had revealed that tablets he'd always felt easy about, because he'd been led to believe they were for his circulation, were in fact heart tablets. 'Heart tablets!' he cried with enfeebled indignation—exactly in the tone he'd used years before when convinced that, having paid one shilling for admission to the cinema, he was sitting in the nine-pennies.

And he was most practical and almost cheerful. Grey and sunken flesh, snoring with pain, pumping a thin choked minimum of breath out of failing lungs. But practical, sensible. I must remember that he'd left money on top of the wardrobe for Mother's instant use. 'When your mother goes, after me, you and Betty must divide things between you.' He was queerly in control, even business-like. 'Well, Ted, you mustn't hang about any longer.' I'd never more strongly felt the oddity of being father and son. I, in health, looked down on him, desperately ill: as long before, the potent man, he'd looked down on me, the sick child. I thought then that we were items in some complex tree, both root and branch—and trunk, leaves, sap. Somehow, for all our terrible differences, we were one, in some inscrutable rhythm of strength and weakness. Each of us was son and father both, in a long paradox of parenthood.

And so, by summoned car, to New Chilton, where I tried gently to suggest that he was awfully ill, my mother must be ready for things to go wrong. But she was unable to imagine such catastrophe. 'I think it'll only be a few days ... Of course, they can do things for him I can't.'

She talked endlessly about her childhood, and the way life had turned drab and dull when she married: no friends, no social life. And soon enough my father had been out night after night enjoying himself while she drudged at home. She had no much-needed new shoes, but he had two suits ... And this was my mother, who'd left her own pitiful home before they'd ever met, because she hadn't wanted to be 'dragged down like that. I didn't see why you had to be.'

In the morning I rang the hospital from a kiosk with a phone that worked. A slight improvement, but as to the future, it was impossible to say what might happen ... And my mother resumed her endless talking. Neighbours: their kindness, and the complicated play this involved, given my father's dread of indebtedness, his readiness to discern ulterior motives in any apparent kindness, and so on. Kindness, for my father, had so often been synonymous with the sinister. So, having hired a car for my visit that evening, I had to apologise to the diabolical persons to one side, and the vile persons to the other; having cunningly suppressed the characteristics attributed to them by my father, they were deeply anxious to drive me to the hospital.

And when I walked into the ward, his gaze was turned already hungrily in the direction from which visitors came. He smiled; for the first time for a great many years, we kissed. He seemed physically no better, but there was a mental vigour that made me suddenly confident that, this time, he wouldn't go. He showed me his scarred belly. That operation the year before had been dreadfully clumsy—it was the ugliest of cuts, a great wrinkling as of amateur stitching with thick, blundering thread.

Poor vain man, so hideously marred!

My mother spoke of the great dismay that operation had been to both of them. They'd thought he was going simply to be cleaned out—he'd be opened and given a kind of light vacuuming. Perhaps he didn't really hear what the specialist said to him when he told my father what was to happen. 'We thought in our silly minds ...' said my mother.

I noted, as I'd done so often during these two days of her relieved flow of talk, how under her uneducated naivety there was this oddly interesting, self-observing, often self-satirising habit of mind. She had a curious comic gift, too—as when talk of my father's stomach led her to talk of her own, and of the approach to it of the surgeon when she'd been in hospital for her own operation. He'd picked it up, the flabby folds of it—'Poor little white tummy!' she exclaimed—and tossed it (she provided the gesture) this way and then (gesture) that. And then he'd gathered it in his hands, 'seeing what shape he could make with it'. She described a more intimate inspection he'd carried out: 'I never knew anyone could put a finger so far!' Then she clapped her hands and cried: 'It's funny with your children!—nice! You spend so long not telling them anything, and then you can tell them whatever you like!'

The whole amusing surprise of life to her was that she and my father had begun their lives in such social misery and deprivation, and were now so comfortable. Being able to buy whatever she wanted was still an ironical amazement to her.

I reached over to take a muscatel from a dish and she cried,

'Oh poor Kate! She so loves nuts and fruit!' As long as I could remember, these inexplicable lamentations on behalf of absent people!

And when he was better, she went down.

There'd been another haemorrhage. So this time she hadn't the leisure—as she'd had, waiting for a previous admission to hospital—to acquire a range of fresh nightwear, complete replacements in the field of toothbrushes, vanity bags, slippers. That time she'd had a heap of nightdresses delivered, to make a choice from. 'Well,' she said, 'it's nicer for the nurses.' She elaborated on this when actually in hospital: 'They hug me and say they've never known a patient with so many pretty nighties.' And she'd been very game, that time. Such a timid woman, who in any real emergency was tough with amusement, interest. 'I never thought,' she'd said, 'that at seventy-five I'd have a ride in an ambulance. I've always wanted that.'

It was one of the words she could never manage—'ambulance': largely because it resisted her usual habit, of substituting a similar but more familiar word. As when she once offered me beer in a choice of 'tanker or beacon'; or boasted of her kindness to a workman who'd come to mend a gas fitting: 'I greeted him with a largo'.

My father was suddenly very, very small and old, with hardly any voice.

We found her in the hospital bed she'd occupied the first time, eight years before: exhausted, her eyes black with trouble. They'd kept her awake all night for blood counts. She was still able to maintain that the ward sister had welcomed her with cries of joy—her favourite patient returned! As for the doctor, he'd asserted that never in a long career had he seen such beautiful skin on an old lady over eighty. 'Incredible!' he had ventured to cry.

She began by being stiff and unsmiling; too uncomfortably alert, like someone in a nest of enemies, to be really at ease with us. Emergencies, as well as bringing out her courage, had always made her tense until she'd mapped out the new situation and setting for herself. I remembered the astonishment of it when I was very small, feeling my warm easy mother suddenly become quite rigid with alarm.

She said, 'The guts and courage of some of the women in here make you feel a coward.'

Then she closed her eyes, and I wondered if she was quite alive, noticing how completely crumpled she now was, the pillars of her neck standing out alarmingly; and then she opened her eyes again and said there was an old lady down the ward who'd been split from here to there, and one of sixty-two who had a boyfriend. In the most appalling extremities she'd never lose her ear for gossip. I'd imagined her among those tumbling festoons of the damned, in a medieval painting, shriekingly on their way to fires and forkings, turning to a fellow tumbler and saying: 'There's an old lady over there who's had seventeen husbands! ...'

She had a curious cause for distress. They'd stapled a plastic bracelet to her wrist, with her name on it. Across nearly half a century it had woken a terrible echo. My brother, his illness wrongly diagnosed, had died on his first birthday, in a London hospital. 'The last time I saw one of these,' said my mother now, 'was on Harry.'

My father had dressed for the visit with great care for her feelings. He was wearing an overcoat, one which he happened to detest, rather than a mackintosh, confident that this would lead to applause for his thoughtfulness. In fact, it brought out her sharpness, the quite bleak scorn she'd always felt free to express if unconvinced by the way someone she loved was dressed. What on earth was he wearing that coat for? He looked so much nicer in his mack!

As we left I said 'Look after yourself', and with that attention to logic and reality she'd displayed throughout, she replied: '*They*'re here to look after me'—meaning the hospital staff. Then she caught at my hand: 'Pray for me!'

On my next visit—I went alone—she was jocular. Being in hospital put her in a position of power, of which very sensibly she took full advantage. She was lovingly scathing about my father: 'I wish he wouldn't keep coming to see if I'm dead.' 'He says he means to come in every day to tell you what he's been doing,' I said. 'Good God,' said my mother; given the strength, she'd obviously have uttered a satirical laugh loud enough to bring the nurses running. 'I don't want to know what he's been *doing*. I want to know what he's been *eating*.'

Yes, it had been the contract between them, as understood

by my mother. For much of their married life, her happiness would have been assured if he'd confined their exchanges to matters of diet, expressions of opinion as to this piece of the breast of English lamb, this cut of pork. All the rest of it, the enormous boredom especially of his paranoiac accounts of office life, she could cheerfully have done without.

I was reminded of the only time when he'd lived away from her, and for more than a year she'd been appallingly uninformed about the food he was eating.

It was early in the war. Suddenly my father was posted away from home, to Trenton, in the Midlands. It was a regional department of the Home Office, and he was to be in charge of ARP and assorted activities of the kind. To my mother's horror—she could see it only as an escapade under an official mask—he opposed a sensible calmness that increased her bewilderment. 'It's wartime, my dear. Have to expect these little inconveniences!' Separation from her husband was not what my mother would have described as a little inconvenience. 'Teddy's here to look after you. There's some things he can do about the house, I suppose. He can look after the allotment. And you can take a lodger. Lots of young clerks looking for digs. Some girl—company for Betty.' His composure, not rashly cheerful but brisk, increased with every suggestion he made. 'And they'll give me a railway pass every third weekend.'

And so, amazingly, he went, and letters came regularly, two a week, full of the same composed, careful satisfaction. He was chairman of the canteen committee. Many of his colleagues were, of course, young idiots, but he had found a crony or two. He had bought a bicycle, for exercise. Tolerable lodgings. His landlady was a fool of a woman, talked too much, but she kept a clean house.

To him my mother wrote every day. Before I set out in the morning, she'd ask me to jot down the spellings of words she'd need for that day's letter. I tried to imagine her end of the correspondence: that tangle of news and views somehow turned into written words. And with the help, I'd reflect, only of the comma. My mother had never mastered the full stop.

We found a girl clerk as a lodger. Heather was plump and deeply conventional; she and I got on badly from the start.

137

About the war she felt much as if it had been a way of scattering her very large family—of brothers, sisters and cousins—in a new and satisfactorily dramatic fashion. It conferred on them more than usual interest. This was a family that spent much of its time relaying, by mail and other means, news of itself to its innumerable members: none of whom, I observed with astonishment, seemed to lack interest in the rest. Their avidity for news was remarkable. Heather was particularly pleased to have cousins in the Royal Air Force. She talked of them as if, for sheer handsomeness, they had been elected to wear the most fascinating of all uniforms. 'He looks terrific in his jacket with those marvellous shoulder flashes,' she confided to Betty in my hearing, speaking of a cousin whose photograph had arrived for positioning on her dressing table. I suppressed an inquiry about the oddity of praising a uniform that qualified its wearer, a pilot, for a short expectation of life. But Heather read the distaste on my face. 'Is there anything wrong in someone looking nice?' she asked with a curiously winsome defiance of which her attitude to me generally consisted. I shrugged. In my diary I noted that she was turning me into an addict of the shrug. 'How else can one respond to her? And her constant offer to tell the story of any film she has seen.' The girls endlessly exchanged the stories of films. I found myself oddly wishing my father was there, to bring these narratives to an end. He had never cared for such bloated synopses.

On the whole I failed to tend the allotment. It became a tiny part of my wartime nightmares, the awareness that this nationally valuable plot was fast returning to the wilderness. Even to keep weeds at bay was a more formidable task than I had ever imagined: from a powdering of green they grew into bold rivals of the plants the plot existed to nourish, and then, overnight it seemed, into its only real crop. When I remembered to go there I felt my unpopularity with those who cared for neighbouring plots. In vegetable language it spoke of treason. I would agitatedly rip out the most impudent weeds, and hunt for discouraged carrots, baffled French beans. One evening my mother came with me, stared about and muttered, 'Terrible! Terrible!' Then she set her handbag down and began to tear at the weeds, with characteristic mild hysteria, seizing them with both hands, again and again nearly toppling backwards as they tore away from the soil. 'I don't know what your father will say.'

We walked home together. The sun was setting on the brow of the town; trees were flooded by a slowly retreating glow, and the church tower was a tall cube of light. I said, 'Isn't it beautiful!' 'Mmm,' said my mother. 'Have you ever thought how nice it is to live under the town and be able to look up at it in the light of the setting sun?' I asked—trying not to remember that along that shining slope a schoolfriend of mine had been blown to pieces by a landmine a few months earlier. 'Hmm.' 'I don't think you're really looking at it,' I teased. 'Oh blast it,' said my mother. 'Oh blast the beauty!'

She had so much to digest inside herself, in my father's absence. Deprived of vital information about his feeding, the condition of his shirts, underwear, pyjamas. And she was worrying, no doubt of it, about what he was generally getting up to, pursuing his blandly satisfactory existence a hundred miles away. She talked to him about this, constantly, inside the busily closed expression on her face; at times her lips actually moved. Once I heard her inner soliloquy rise to the surface: 'It's all right for you ...' she muttered. She also had the daily news to rehearse for him. Now that he was no longer on the other side of the supper table, giving his impatient half-attention to her account of the day's doings—intrinsically so much more interesting than his predictable talk about the office—she had to conduct the conversation, in her head, for both of them. Her deepest expressions of gloom, I suspected, marked her perfectly realistic instinct as to what he'd say, to this or that item of news or opinion. My father lived in his wife's head with a reality even more insistent than when he'd been present in the flesh. It seemed likely that his power grew even greater: she was able more easily to imagine him tetchy than to imagine him relaxed.

But now, thirty years later, she was suddenly sent home. There was a new attitude to the diet she'd staunchly stuck to since her original operation for diverticulitis. It was now agreed that such a diet, dreadfully bland, gave the bowels too little to do. A lover of food who'd painfully learned to tell herself that she was indifferent to much of it, she now had to become a modified lover of food again.

139

But she was vastly disappointed to have been turned out. It was as if she'd been snatched away from a theatre after the first scene of a play. She'd been ready to immerse herself deeper and deeper in the affairs of her fellow-sufferers. She was enjoying the status of oldest lady in the ward.

No, said my father. She couldn't have the assembly of her family that she now dreamed of, to celebrate her return home. She must rest. Mother didn't want to rest: but there was nothing she could do. It was exactly as when he informed her that she no longer wanted her 'picture papers'—a daily and then a Sabbath tabloid. She hadn't the time to read them, he said, and he cancelled them, leaving mother wistfully bereft. Perhaps his shows of power when she came back from hospital rested on his impatience at the importance conferred on her by the sheer fact of being in hospital. Certainly, my sister said, as an eyewitness—on his last visit, benign though he'd set out to be throughout the episode, he'd not been able to refrain from disputing her disputable statements. He'd even decided not to let one of her verbal inventions pass unreproved. She'd had a bath, she said, and they'd 'put a satchel in it.' 'You mean "sachet," ' he said testily. 'I don't care what I mean,' she said. 'It was very nice.'

She had, of course, to be brought to order.

But I was glad she was back at home. Fear for her would not now be among the nervousnesses I'd take with me to West Africa.

PART FOUR

1

I walked: first in one direction, past a strangely sombre fishing village. Its huts had roofs of despondent grey; in the green brilliance of the coconuts they seemed, for all that they were very visible, to be skulking. No one was to be seen; it was odd to feel, in this general brightness, so grey a silence. Yet how much of my impression of silence was due to my being so extreme a stranger?

The beach was overgrown with a succulent whose flower was like morning glory's, but lilac-coloured, and in all directions it sent out tendrils of astonishing length. I walked yard after disbelieving yard in search of the end of one of these, its petering out at last in some casual blast of blossom half-buried in the sand ...

Then I turned the other way, in the direction of the white fort built by the Portuguese a dozen years before Columbus sailed across the Atlantic. As I walked, the coconut trees crackled around me: a sound, to my European ear, like atmospherics on radio. The air itself seemed to be splintering. At intervals I saw women breaking rocks into stones, chippings, of various sizes. Then I was among the fishermen, a thickening of boats drawn up on the sand: curved, carved, vivaciously coloured, with long names sprawling along their prows. I was among children, who called at me, and after me, mischievously. I felt a clown: Hallo, they called, and Good morning, and How do you do? It was a world of parody: I was a parody Englishman. A penny? they cried, also, and formed little petitionary tails to my passage.

Among the fishermen I seemed never to have been among humans so black, so glistening. They gleamed under the sun, and I had an abject sensation of being, as it were, quite unreflecting. The sun ignored me. I came closer and closer to

143

the fort. The sea was fringed with human dung. Activity thickened: fishermen black and chatting over their boats, shining naked children sitting in the water with the effect of being in the only possible place; women everywhere with loaded heads. It was, for the jabber and shine of it, a holiday beach in Europe—but it was a working beach in Africa. I realised with amusement that I had never imagined a working beach that had the colour, tone, chattering excitement—that infants' playground sound—of a beach used for idle pleasure.

And I realised that I was, as never before, among Africans. Heaven knew where the nearest European was. Alice in Wonderland was as deeply estranged from familiarity as she'd ever been. I was now at the peak of the village, where the fort stood, its white solidity most curiously irrelevant. It was as if some fishing village in England had had the Tower of London imposed upon it. Here the boats ran in from the open sea, to a species of maritime slip-road. Under those great white walls they darted, casual works of art. Here, on the beach, fishermen were busy disentangling their nets, straightening them, beige or blue, over forests of planted stakes. I stood at the centre of the village and tried to take in this unfamiliar panorama of labour.

But—thank God!—I was out of my depth. I was marvellously lost.

I turned into the village, the main street leading back towards the university hostel where I was staying. It had been a Portuguese town, with houses ornate, wooden; heavy carved outer stairways. They had been gnawed by centuries of occupation. Whole storeys had vanished. The town had been used and used in an infinity of use. There was the substance of it, the old Portuguese houses, and there was the debris: cartons, packing cases, every kind of fragment, made to serve over and over again.

Everywhere, amazing movement: intricate coming and going. Everywhere, delicately-treading chickens. Mercy Stores: the Famous Glass Cutters: House $6\frac{3}{4}$. An old man strolled towards me, over his shrunken shoulder a midnight blue cloth, under his arm, a formal rolled umbrella. Naked children darted in and out of heaps of vividly stained earth. In Aggie's Music Bar an ancient record revolved, filling the air with a thin cackle of unsuitable music. Jack Buchanan, was it? I walked through it all, feeling the absurdity of attempting to look at home in the midst of so much astonishment. How foolish it was, I thought, to be so different. Never in my life had I been so amazingly foreign to my surroundings ...

Oh God! The agony and pleasure of discovering that human beings could be so unalike! And in historical terms, the madness of it! Could the terminal perils of the late twentieth century really spring from a failure to enjoy these deeply agreeable human dissimilarities?

My trip had begun with these few days in Ghana, and I'd come to Cape Coast to interview a novelist. It had been wonderfully difficult, getting here at all. That is, from Accra, where arrangements for the journey should have been made by friendly broadcasters. They were friendly, indeed, but not, I discovered, the best arrangers of journeys. My particular friend, into whose hands Jenny Mallet had confided me, would sit with me in his office, tapping his desk with a pencil, smiling; for long periods quite silent; at times touching a button on the desk that brought BBC voices into the room. The afternoon before my visit to Cape Coast I'd sat there, wondering if this gentle, unbelievably unassertive man might vary this routine with some actual reference to my plans. He did not do so. In the end I had to say:

'Ah! Going to Cape Coast, tomorrow, as you know. As arranged. Hmm! Transport ...'

Unfortunately, he said—and I do believe he would have said nothing at all had I not obliged myself to raise the issue—no car was available. It would be necessary to go by bus.

Ah! I said: and where, and when, was the bus to be found and boarded?

Ah! he said. Well, it probably would be at the bus station, and it might be at seven or eight in the morning. Or half past six. Some such time. He touched the button and we listened for some minutes to a World Service talk on, I think, porcelain. 'You don't know exactly when?' I asked, believing this to be a species of button touched, too: surely he'd at once rush around, at the very least pick up the telephone, and

145

make inquiries. He would, let us say, *get in touch with the bus company.*

No, unfortunately, he said, he was not in possession of this information ...

In the end my host—I was staying with a friend—rang State Transport, rang my destination, arranged that he and a cousin should go to town before six o'clock, and the cousin would queue for a ticket, and Joe would return to the house and fetch me. The bus would depart at 7.15.

And so it happened—except for that detail about the time of departure. We sat, tight-packed, in the already great heat, for an hour, while the intention to get going took shape. A seller of bibles and tracts took the opportunity to come aboard and circulate, with some success, among us. 'You can use them,' he cried, holding his wares aloft as if being in mid-air added to their attractiveness, 'for your X-mas books—your X-mas presentations.' He made with particular eagerness the case for buying a book on How to Use the Psalms. It was, to my ear, Sums. 'Learn how to use the Sums! It is a very nice and essential book.' I thought, as I thought of so many speakers in Africa, that I wanted him not to be at the mercy of his displaced understanding of the genius of the English language. I wanted him not to yoke the words 'nice' and 'essential.' I thought again how all this English was a clumsy mask, under which the true quick man or woman, the one using the tongue he or she had grown up with, was curiously hidden, stowed away. It was like the parody of the Western city that every African city had turned into. We had obliged Africa to spend much of its time in appalling parody. I tried to imagine a London barrowboy required to cry his wares in Fanti, or Chi ...

And such a beautiful, uncomfortable journey. I had never been so aware of the discomfort of having a behind and legs. I could have been very happy without them. Because I was hemmed in, in this great heat, my bottom seemed to swell, to become inordinate. I was a tiny, tortured personality mounted on this immense aching bottom.

But beautiful! The beaches especially, when we reached the coast. They were the subject of much painful local art, but I didn't know anyone who'd caught it, the truth of the scene: the glittering and tumbling sea viewed through the stems of the coconuts as they leaned this way and that; the tangle of light and shade created by those stems; the curved boats being dashed upwards on foaming scrolls of water, and the coloured crowds striving to master the wild things, or hauling on lines.

What a shore it was! Old forts; tumbled villages falling down from, or down to, the beach; the rusty mud of huts and the other omnipresent rust of corrugated iron; everywhere incredibilities of colour. Numb and physically wretched, I was, after all, enormously happy ...

The novelist I was interviewing was the headmaster of one of the schools for which this coast was famous. 'Given over', as a friend in London had prepared me to find, 'to the education industry.' It was here that a poet I'd dined with a night or two earlier had been educated, and had learned, he said, to be grateful for English as the language that presented him with richer resources than any other of which he had knowledge. A poetic pirate, Michael—short only of a cutlass—huge-framed, in a voluminous white half-gown and three-quarter-length trousers striped with pink, black and white. The discussion that evening, over and after dinner, had been mostly about language. A small intelligent broadcaster, who chanced to be the son of a king, thought that, for an African, writing in English could only be an approximation. Real African literature lay in the speech of the custodian of the court: in the untranslateable phrasings of the popular tongue. 'You don't have to come to find African writers,' he said. 'They have found themselves. They have always been here.' A quick intense speaker, whose hands flowed as he talked.

Michael said that was all very well, but we were talking about *written* literature. And was there to be no access to ... *Hamlet?* Michael as a schoolboy, everyone said, had been a great—at least a most sonorous—Prince of Denmark. Impossible not to believe that: his voice was like the ringing of some deep bell. The broadcaster was amazed that anyone should speak of ... what was it? ... *Hamlet.* What had this old alien text to offer compared with the living dramas enacted daily, and always aptly phrased, in the local courts? Oh curse, he said, these grammar schools on Cape Coast, that filled useful men with other people's stale ideas. Michael laughed

147

hugely, every note sounding in the belfry of his vocal cords. Well, the Arts Council of Ghana, of which the other was a member, should cease holding open competitions for literary work. 'All you ever get is the trash.' Instead they should use their funds to publish writers whose work was known to be good—though as things were it rarely got into print. Not, at any rate, into local print.

And another guest, the neat, trim-suited George, expressed the view of language of the well-educated political scientist he was, admirer of the prose styles of Harold Laski and John Strachey. If one learned English it must be in order to command it in the manner of an Englishman. I thought of George's fear for his books, his papers. He was already in trouble, as someone who'd returned to Ghana after the fall of Nkrumah, and was trying to carry out an impossible task: to organise political education, officially, whilst, equally officially, all political activity was forbidden. The ultimate difficulty was that he couldn't move lightly and quickly, for those very papers and books of his. 'I value my newspaper cuttings, pamphlets, books, notes, more than any money I might ever earn,' he'd told me. He could never bring himself to flee without the help of a pantechnicon.

And I thought how painful it must be, to attempt to apply a political outlook based on the study of Western specialists to the raw melodrama, dashed with farce, of political life in a country newly independent. George was often lost in worry, as he might well be. His enemies, he thought, were inefficient enough to take any steps against him, however irrational. At times—and thinking especially of his wife and children—he wondered if it was worth it. Essentially, Army, Police and Civil Service needed reform. And anyone who said the reform of these bodies was his aim—and really, he'd spent years of study qualifying himself to say just this—would never achieve power ...

Well, he'd taken me in Accra to Job 600, the towering building erected in eleven months for a meeting of the Organisation of African Unity, in Nkrumah's last days: eighteen workmen had died in the helter-skelter of it, George said. At its monumental feet, the tiny neatness of the old colonial State House. All those suites, sixty of them, lavish, unfinished: a palace interrupted in the last stages of its

148

extravagant embellishment. And from the great windows, such a view of the city ... where it looked, here, there, everywhere, as if whole villagefuls of people had been incongruously packed into decaying side streets ...

When I'd interviewed my headmaster-novelist, he drove me to the university hostel on the beach, and told me over lunch how ambiguous was his view of the parody of nineteenth-century English public school education in which he was involved—*Tom Brown's Schooldays* with food riots added, these hungry violences being virtually part of the school calendar. Like the poet Michael, he was grateful for much the system offered: but thought it had done harm to Ghanaian society, in producing so ... oh yes, inappropriate ... an elite.

His laughter was like Michael's, a different range of bells, but still most bell-like, merry. Well, he said, they'd had it easy here, really—so much easier altogether in West Africa than in East Africa ...

And I was totally wet with sweat, could have sworn I heard the sound of it pouring down my skin. Undressing, I was wearily amused by the struggle to remove a shirt: it was like stripping long-established wallpaper. In the hostel there was no fan, no air conditioning, and I woke again and again to find myself a pond in the general lake of the bed.

And so I rose early—to a scene absolutely bewitching. The sea had been turned to quicksilver. Spread across it, motionless, black, filled with tiny black figures, were fishing boats. The scene had enormous silvery depth, on which the sun was just beginning to splash its blazing gold. The boats looked like splinters in a silver skin. In some sense, air and water were one, a single silver waiting to be gilded.

It was a dream, but real. And across the water sounded the bells of the fishermen's voices, the tumbling peals of their laughter.

2

I breakfasted alone, wishing I liked goat's milk, or the taste of
the bread, which I found sickly. A car called and bore me to
the studios. The sun had set the air alight: we moved through
flames. I presented the chit admitting me to the studios to a
sleepy soldier, whose rifle, with fixed bayonet, rested against
the wall behind him. I interviewed a playwright and a critic,
and was appalled by the dimness of my voice. It sounded like
my father's when he was last in hospital.

Could I survive four more weeks in this oven of West
Africa? What had Richard Burton said of Lagos—my next
stop? 'A coffin wherein is found annually a dead consul.' If
he'd not died of disease, the poor diplomat would have
melted away, even his bones becoming a steaming sort of
liquid.

But happenings, surely, meetings with people, would act as
buoyancy tanks?

George's daughter, born in England, three years old, talked
like a tiny manuscript—or like someone editing a manuscript: so that if, starting with a singular verb, she discovered
her subject was plural, she went back to the beginning and
changed the verb. We played catchball under George's
frangipani trees, but I felt I was being rather frivolous in the
presence of some Principal of Girton, who simply happened
to be much smaller than was the custom with that office-
holder ...

I was taken to see a playwright who appeared, through a
central doorway, and with a handmaiden in attendance, to
where Joe and I had been waiting, in some sort of outdoor
cloister. It was all designed, Joe whispered, like a chief's
courtyard. It was audience we were granted. She said
government was otherness in Africa, and had been so since

150

colonial days. It was still uncertain how you restored to people their simple confidence in the right to be their own governors. In the theatre, she herself set out to discover if she was genuine. That was the general African search—for its own honesty. It had been provided with so many means of being false. Generalising splendidly, she said she did not like generalisations; she did not like talk; she liked action: and theatre was action. 'I like answer-finding people,' she said, and smiled beautifully. She then gave me a photograph of herself.

I prepared to fly to Nigeria. At times, I had to confess —well, when finding that an interview with a playwright had become an audience with a queen—I felt I ought to give up this African interest of mine. Oh, Africa was immense, and immensely baffling. I surely hadn't the various sorts of sturdiness required if you were really to have any hope of understanding it.

I found my head was full, appreciatively, of the fundamental cries you saw painted on the mammy trucks, the lorries that filled the broken roads. You Lie; Save me, Oh God; Abomination; Think on that Day. I was sustained, somehow, by the general fervour of these exclamations, which raced towards you at, roughly speaking, seventy miles an hour ...

3

Save me Oh God, indeed. I should have been in Kano, in northern Nigeria; here I was in a hotel in Lagos, five hundred miles short of my target.

Joe and Michael had seen me off—in Accra's VIP lounge: it was the first and last time I'd be in such a place—and, a kind of walking waterfall, dripping with sweat, I'd gone across to the aeroplane and so arrived, wetter yet, in Lagos. But the flight had been retimed, in some very quiet fashion, without reference to passengers or their aims in respect of connections and so forth, so my flight onwards to Kano had gone: and here I was, in the Airport Hotel, waiting for the afternoon plane.

The war with Biafra had increased the nervous tensions of arrival. As was technically correct, I'd noted my profession on the immigration form as 'Author.' The young officer who read it was pardonably puzzled by this assertion. I wrote books? Then I must tell him what they were called. I wished at once that I'd written books with sensible titles: I'd gladly have been the authors of *War and Peace, Middlemarch, Martin Chuzzlewit.* How silly it now seemed to have written books that no one had advised me against calling *Shrieking Boys, These Foolish Lads, A Cross-Eyed War.* I recited these titles miserably, and was then, but in a half-hearted fashion, admitted to the country, in the wake of a Ghanaian who'd brought his own food, in the form of appetising-looking meat balls, dozens of them, every one of which he was made to break into useless fragments, to demonstrate that they contained no forbidden ingredient.

I lay all day in my hotel bedroom wondering why I had brought upon myself this curious and drastic discomfort, which consisted in the absence of all that was familiar by way of temperature, taste and behaviour ...

And in the late afternoon we were driven back to the airport, which was a scene of multiple confusion. There'd been some original intention of confusing things, which had been over-ruled as totally inadequate by some advanced experts in confusion, who'd then been ousted by their superiors—though none of these specialists had actually retired from the field. On all sides I was asked for 'dash', on grounds difficult to resist. In brief, and as a model, a sum of money to this smiling fellow would ensure that your luggage was put on the plane, rather than being subjected to some degrading ceremony of destruction at unspecified hands; and another sum of money to this possessor of a menacing grin would ensure that the activities of the fellow with the smile were monitored, and steps taken if they should threaten to deviate from the action agreed.

In the departure lounge, rumour had it that something had gone wrong with the plane itself. It was possible to check on this by staring out at a Fokker Friendship that had clearly fallen below standard in respect of the wiring in one of its wings. I had not realised that wings contained miles—tangled miles—of wire. Hugely laughing technicians, balancing on strangely amateurish-looking ladders, were pulling out such wire, and stuffing it back again. Their laughter seemed to me to be that of men as surprised as I was to learn there was wire inside the wings of aeroplanes. Having made the discovery, there was nothing to do but stuff the wire back, in a rough-and-ready way, whilst laughing. You were perhaps laughing at the idea of such an aeroplane attempting to fly to Kano.

But for all that, my God, just before the hour at which the wartime ban on flying at night came into effect, we were away. In a misty sundown, we were crawling above forest that was inset with villages—from that height, resembling ceramic brooches, shapes of rough terracotta. With darkness, these turned into tiny blazing worms, wrinkles of fire. Inside the plane it was, remarkably, rather chilly ...

And Kano. No one waiting. A town, when we drove through it in the airways minibus, unlike any I'd ever been in. No street lights, but many kinds of fire along the roadside, and lanterns, and smoke making a paler night, and light guttering and blowing and streaming, or snapping into flower in some unexpected quarter, or suddenly blooming silver or smoky blue instead of gold. The smell of the smoke seemed to stream and billow, too. It was, on a grand scale, much like my bedroom when I was sick, as a child, and they'd lit a fire, and the flames took leaping bites at the darkness. Ravishing, I thought, light as a wandering soft various thing, to someone used to electricity. And everywhere, movement: but difficult to interpret, figures sliding in and out of flame.

The whole town was talking to itself, at the top of its voice, and there seemed to be horsemen.

I had this address: 444 Dan Ugundi. Yes, said the minibus driver, looking quite unbaffled: yes—he'd never heard of it, but would ... Not saying what he would do, he did it— dropped me in the street, though it seemed not so much a street as a corner torn out of some huge scene: a fitful angle, roaring and full of robes and teeth, from which emerged a taxi-driver.

He did not speak English, but smiled, to make up for it. He would be glad if I held on to the door of the cab, he indicated, since it was about to fall off. His smile became rueful. Then we drove away, towards Dan Ugundi. Which I saw as a street, obviously a long street, with No. 1 at one end, and No. 444 at the other.

It wasn't like that at all. We entered, by way of bucketing and surging—touch seemed to have been lost with some vital principle of the internal combustion engine—a sprawling, smoky world: with great trees set in it, at random. It was *A Midsummer Night's Dream,* grown amazingly dusty. There were houses, but they were scattered, and had the character of minor Arab castles. As we rattled into a courtyard, what appeared to be a gown thrown on the ground leapt to its feet and revealed itself as a watchman, complete with sword. I felt a long way from home. This was not Hertfordshire. Or had I lost my wits—was I imagining it all? It was, I thought, the sort of thing I *would* imagine ...

The walls of the houses, if they *were* houses, were of red mud, sloped and curved, and seemed to be without doors. Absolutely no familiar method of inquiry offered itself. My aching mumble of '444 Dan Ugundi?' evoked from watchmen only flashing smiles or flashing scowls. I wondered uneasily about the circumstances in which the sword might be used.

My stomach ached, horribly. I hadn't eaten for nearly twelve hours. My voice was going. The world through which we blundered seemed more and more smokily implausible. My driver, tall in his gown, was not so much a pillar of strength as a pillar of ... pity. His huge eyes seemed bright with tears.

It was a mad game: of watchmen leaping to their feet; of heads shaken; and my driver surely about to blubber, amid such an absence of knockers and doorbells as I couldn't have dreamt of. And almost the worst of it was that every ten minutes or so we'd wander into someone on a bicycle. It would gleam, the bicycle, brighter surely than when new, except for certain parts, always including the crossbar, wrapped in corrugated paper. Later I discovered it was thought stylish to retain the packing the machine had arrived in, and if it was lost, or missing, actually to purchase packing, so as not to be the owner of a mere naked bike ... We'd stop, the engine of the cab sounding as if none of its components had ever been connected to any other—*that* was the trouble; all the bits had been thrown under the bonnet and never joined up—and I'd croak my inquiry: '444 Dan Ugundi?'

Cyclists were unlike watchmen: they always gave confident, charming replies. They'd point—at what I came to see was courteous random: and, having no better advice to fall back on, we'd turn in that direction ... to be a cause of fury to yet more sword-waving watchmen ...

The end came when to a slender young man—he looked like an Arab poet, or perhaps the secretary to a great philosopher—I mentioned the name of the British Council officer who, London held, lived at 444 Dan Ugundi. He thought he could lead us to it, and did so. We'd been there already, and the watchman had been more than usually unwelcoming. But this was it, certainly, said the young man ... and I looked into a lighted room: and there were English chairs, in the revived nineteenth-century style familiar to so many British school staff-rooms; and there, even more clinchingly, was a marmalade cat. No one was at home. The young man convinced the watchman of my legitimacy; and I climbed into a Land Rover standing against the house as a shelter from the long-past-midnight scream of mosquitoes.

The Mahons, when they arrived—they'd given me up, and had gone to an all-night cinema—were astonished to find they were living at 444 Dan Ugundi. It was an address totally unfamiliar to them—though they made no fuss about believing that, technically, that was where they lived.

It was a little sawn-off sort of night, and at once I was in a teachers' training college, talking about African literature. My voice vanished in the closing moments, like the last eddies of bathwater disappearing down a plughole. Dumb, I went on a tour of the town, this marvellous apotheosis—I thought—of the mud-pie. Best of all, the dye works—pits and ditches in the red earth in which indigo was extracted—attended by men and women and boys who were all, in one degree or another, indigo-stained. Indigo boys grinned at me, indigo grins; a man trotted towards me on indigo legs; a young woman was beautifully indigo of arm and shoulder.

But just as good, when it came to it, was the market. I was accompanied by a brisk woman from the British Council, who was much like my favourite teacher at Barley Road Elementary School, forty years before. It was the nearest I'll ever get to the sensation of being in a medieval market, and there I was, amid all that colour and movement, among such smells, and such heaps of rice and potato, such painted little girls, and girls and boys masked and singing, and others with their faces polka-dotted; and among such heaps of coloured clothes, and embroidered shoes, and lamps made of milk tins, and every possible aid to horsemanship: brilliant saddles, horse masks, spurs—things designed to make the horse as gaudy as its rider ... there I was, in such a setting, and there was my companion, as sensible as Miss Baker at Barley Road had been, and great at bargaining, so that when my heart was set on unimaginable waistcoats for my sons, Tom and Dan, she didn't allow me to buy them by any direct method. And her bargaining, indeed, was so indirect that, what with our walking away and being pursued and positively dragged back, and expressions on both sides of the certainty of ruination if the purchase were completed, it was half an hour before we came to the end of it.

And being reminded of Miss Baker meant that I was reminded also of the view of Africa I'd been given at Barley Road, a sentimental view of savages, on the whole; and I felt furtive, a little, there in Kano, wondering if that old education might show in my face.

I wished I were to be longer in this town with its open spaces filled with dust and people, its mounds and pyramids of sacks of groundnuts; and the superb horsemen seen cantering through gates, down vistas of the inescapable dust. But I had to go off to talk again, at a girls' school; and then, having ground almost to a halt, my voice a few harsh fragments of sound, to a dinner, where I couldn't bring myself to eat—even making my way through an ordinary meal had begun to feel like some athletic ordeal of Olympic size—but where I felt an exhausted affection for my fellow-guests, among them a shy Hausa who crouched low over his plate and used his fork according to some beautiful awkward principle I could not understand, and a Fulani with the most delicate of features, all writers, longing to be published and read.

156

4

And there I was, the next day, being driven the hundred or so miles south to Zaria. The astonishing thing about this was that the great bush through which the road was driven—step into it, Bill Mahon said, and you were as good as being in Ethiopia; he meant, that's where it was uninterruptedly headed—was like Windsor Great Park, gone faintly mad. It was essentially trim, though on a vast scale: an enormous wild tidiness. We crossed bridges over rivers as wide as the Thames in London, but the rivers had gone. There was sand only. It didn't seem possible that a river could have been so substantial and have dried up. There was cotton, and lilac flowers of the sugar-cane, and houses whose domed roofs had turned blood red with the peppers spread out on them to dry; and far away in that flat aboriginal parkland, like remote anachronisms, gowned figures on bicycles. By the roadside, a car that had been rashly quitted; it was being swarmed over by men who, Bill said, would within minutes have reduced it to its various parts, and borne those parts off into the secret bush. They'd be unlikely to leave a patch of oil for the owner.

Touching these great towns of northern Nigeria—being, even for a moment, part of their dust and hurly-burly and brilliantly decorated mud—was like any fine experience occurring too quickly: it dazzled me and made me angry, and I was angrier when I came to rest in Kaduna, which, by comparison with the others, is dull, European. But I was happy there, all the same. For it was there that I conducted what was grandly called a Television Workshop. It was to be an exercise in writing dramatically. Faced with a roomful of attractive northern faces, robes, embroidered caps, I quickly invented the art of television drama, and we chose to work on a Hausa form of the story of Death and the Merchant. I went

157

off then to record a discussion on TV Kaduna on The Nigerian Dramatist.

And so, at the end of such staggeringly colourful days, the experience of colourlessness: my own face, in that evening's transmission, dreadfully pale, the lighting being adjusted to black skin, and very thin, so much of me sweated away. If I'd been asked to respond to a roll-call, I couldn't honestly have replied 'Present'. There was that sensation I always disliked when watching myself, of being made aware of my outwardness. That expression you'd always thought was an amiable smile turned out to be a foolish smirk. Indignantly, you noticed that you had false teeth. How had that happened?

But the British Council representative in Kaduna, to my delight, said he liked visiting specialists (that was the technical word) to be offbeat, to contradict the familiar tidy British image. I couldn't help being pale, and smirking, but I could very easily avoid being tidy.

My son Dan, who was opposed to the familiar *junior* British image, as of a keeper of hamsters and rabbits, had asked me to bring back a vulture. I saw one thoughtfully perched on a roof overlooking the bathing-pool behind my hotel, and wished Dan were there to see it, too. Kaduna, as this view across the pool made curiously clear, was flat and trim, without the beautiful muddle and bustle of Kano and Zaria. Its teacher training college seemed similarly flat. I was to talk there about books and reading, in the most general way, but the English Language Officer had warned me that the vocabulary of my audience was small. I found myself faced with great numbers of astonishingly buxom girls in yellow and green school dresses, and young men in white shirts. I was suddenly very tired indeed, could hardly put one word in front of another, and was very worried that any words I chose might be unfamiliar. Hoarsely I retreated from word to word; and so fell back (as on late winter days in the school where I'd taught in London) on grinning ...

Lord, the TV-drama workshop was worthwhile. I'd thought it might turn out to be an absurd luxury. Why wasn't it simple *radio* drama? But the quality of the work swept all doubt away. They went off and wrote, and came back and gave solo performances of the scenes they'd written; and there

158

was the intentness I'd sometimes known as a teacher, individual concentration becoming the shared absorption of a group. They worried their way into that old story, of the merchant who thinks to cheat Death by leaving ... in this version, Kano for Zaria: Death having been privately astonished to see him in Kano, in the first place, since he had an appointment with him elsewhere tonight. In Zaria, of course.

A young Englishman, on voluntary service, had been horribly injured in a road accident, and lay desperately ill in the local hospital as we worked. We were mopping up at the end of a day when the news came that he'd not won his battle with death. There would have been grief, I guess, anyway, because we'd all been caught up in *that* struggle; but as one of the young writers said, after a long silence, it was because we'd been so raptly concerned with the theme of human mortality that this news was heard with such sharp sorrow.

5

It was the merest intermission, I was to be overworked to the end, but here I was on one of the great beaches in Lagos, in swimming shorts and the thinnest possible shirt; and the Atlantic, my Cornish marvel, had here become an African marvel, armies of white lions springing and snapping at the sand, and tumbling over one another with a roar of snowy manes. The sand was white, too; the sea patched with gold and plum-red. Little crabs, looking like the ghosts of crabs, popped out of holes. Night came like some clever instant change of scene: Look, it's day!—Oh no, it's night! In the warm and busy dusk, the beach religions were active around their little sandy churches. Cherubim and Seraphim danced their holy highlife, a marvellous unity of sacred and profane; they sang to the stars, a congress of Ella Fitzgeralds and

Mahalia Jacksons, and prepared for dawn and great extravagances of baptism. In ragged and flickering bright holes in the night made by the light from oil lamps, themselves made from milk tins—each hole a trader's stall—Harry and his wife Joanna chose their fish, from a variety of great silver monsters.

Harry was the British Council representative in Lagos, and happily, serviceably, I thought, had a touch and more of hedonism about him. It was not going to be like East Africa. I should not have to make a tramp's face to counter the respectable faces of my hosts.

The trouble—which had begun in the north, and was scheduled to continue here—was going to be buffet suppers.

If I'd died—and I certainly thought I should—the verdict, if it had not been death by excessive lecturing, might well have been death by buffet supper. I endured eleven of these events in a row. Inwardly—and very nearly outwardly—snoring, miserably clutching glass and plate, I'd feign to lend an ear to the totally local discussions that were occurring around me. My being in Lagos was an excuse for these discussions to occur. I was the virtually anonymous guest of honour. Exhausted, I was, in the very nature of the buffet supper, required to stand. To say that I longed to sit would be untrue: I longed to lie down. I longed to give myself up frankly to the coarsest kind of sleep. I could not imagine sleep unaccompanied by vulgar blasts of snoring. The more refined the buffet supper, the more disgusting my ideal of sleep.

One increasing problem was that I really didn't understand what was being said to me. It wasn't only the enormous noise that reigned on such occasions. It was a kind of panic of the ears. 'Meet my friend Mince Pie,' my companion would seem to say. And then, leaning towards the newcomer: 'How long have you been mad?' Or she would tell me of her current circumstances. 'Scriabin' (her husband?) 'is nitpicking in the Tiddlies.' (Desperately I'd tell myself that I knew where they were: islands off the west coast of … somewhere.) 'He's' (huge roar of laughter from behind us) 'but I always say' (enormous laughter from in front of us) 'more or less fiddly or sesquipedalian' (I'd hear with the greatest clarity a full minute of

160

political talk from a group a whole room distant) 'but what do you think?'

Worst of all was the problem of African names, in respect of which I'd become, in most other contexts, very calm. 'You must come and meet,' someone would seem to say, 'Frank the Jeweller.'

'Oh, yes.'

'He's married to Oboe Umbilicus, whom you know, of course.'

'Ah.'

' ... he's locally adipose ...'

'Ah, yes.'

' ... rich acts of circumcision ...'

'I see.'

' ... farted in chains at ... with nobs on ...'

'My goodness.'

'So I'll goose you, Tim.'

'Pardon?'

'He's over here, I think.' He isn't, but we make one of those attempts at an encounter that punctuate these parties and give them their gritty general flavour of failure, and are somewhat more exacting than playing Rugby football at international level.

An effect of all this was that I became aware of a loss of sensation between my right thigh and knee. This area of my body ceased, at buffet suppers, to exist. It was dreadfully absent when I attended one in the garden of the British High Commission. The moon lay on the water of the harbour; the trees and bushes were full of the vivacious conversation of insects—which had the special virtue that I was not required to take part in it. Immense fragrances drifted around, indiscriminately offering pleasure. There was tension at this party: a messenger from the British Prime Minister had arrived with some communication that could not have been unimportant; he was here, in the garden, and the very insects seemed to converse at a higher pitch than usual. I drifted into the power of a young official who confessed that he knew nothing about African writing, but did not allow that to prevent him from having the firmest opinions about it, all expressed in the bureaucratic subjunctive. 'I would have thought ...' Knowing nothing about African writing, he

161

would have thought it might be in difficulties, because English was so hospitable, but at the same time so treacherous. You could choose the wrong word, in English, with enormous confidence, and come an enormous cropper. He, at any rate, would have thought that this was the situation. He would also have thought that Nigerians were in special difficulty, having vernaculars, he gathered, of great vigour. And much else he would have thought, and quite unsubjunctively *did* say. I myself would have thought that the moon was wilting.

It was at this point that my malaise spread across my frame. I was face to face with a serious problem. Was it possible that gangrene of the private parts could set in and complete its dreadful mission within a single evening? My imagination had no difficulty in deciding that it could. I longed to chafe these unfortunate items back to life before it was too late, but could see that this would strain even Harry's tolerance. I spent the crux of the evening attempting to reconcile myself to a future without genitals. I had little success in this.

Actually, something like the resuscitatory process I'd had in mind was offered, when not needed at all, on the evening when Harry took us to a night club.

It had been a shattering day. One of my purposes in being in Nigeria was to persuade teachers and others that children might read for pleasure and not have betrayed their fundamental aim in life, which was to read for obvious studious ends.

Nigeria brimmed with bookshops—The Supreme Bookshop, The World's Greatest Bookshop, The Knowledgeable Bookshop ... Many had blackboards displayed outside, on which were noted recently-arrived titles. They were Treadmill's Algebra, Books I-VI; Yawn and Slumber's English Grammar; Twitch's Shorthand; Groan's Elementary Surveying. There was never a piece of fiction so welcomed and announced; never a work of imagination of any kind.

Well, clearly, in a society where it seemed to offer the only way forward, education was likely to be taken very seriously. The problem, equally clearly, is that a very odd human being may be produced by a literary diet confined to textbooks. In

162

any case, the imagination is not a passenger, when it comes to equipping yourself with algebra, shorthand, surveying elementary or advanced, grammar. The child whose imagination has been nourished is likely to manage those disciplines better, not worse, than one whose imagination has been neglected.

And anyway—how awful to contemplate a generation deprived of stories ...

The British Council had set out with a wholly admirable disingenuousness to demonstrate the virtue of imaginative reading. They had—and this is where the whole educational world would have been obliged to say 'Ahem!'—tested the general educational capacity of pupils in selected schools in Lagos. They had then sent out to these schools boxes full of books. They were not textbooks. The schools were asked to see that the books were read. After which the Council's education officers re-tested the children concerned. Hurrah! A statistically detectable improvement in performance!

There would have been blushes in Heaven—but cheers as well. The real problem, I thought when I saw the book boxes, was that, of the books chosen, most—fairly inevitably—were intended for European consumption. They reflected a wholly white world. Where they didn't, there could be difficulties. A book about life in Ghana was accused of containing immoral pictures. It turned out to have a photograph or two of tiny boys playing, naked.

And the real problem lying behind *that* real problem, it seemed to me, was that Nigeria as yet had no children's literature. I talked about this with publishers' representatives in Lagos, and they were all convinced that any attempt to publish such books would be ruinous. Well, there was no habit of reading for pleasure, and little money to spare for buying books that would seem dispensable. But I thought the ultimate health of publishing itself in Africa might depend on it. If there was no child audience for general reading now, what adult audience would there be in ten or twenty years' time? ...

But I was there to press the value of reading for pleasure, and I'd done it all that day, in school after school, feeling impertinent, somewhat, but buoyed up by a shameless belief in what I was saying, and usually by the nature of my audience. I've always had a tendency to fall in love with audiences—there must be a word for it—and I was specially susceptible to some of these, buzzing, confused, amiable, in the midst of such humming dustiness and damp. I understood, indeed, as my own frame fell to pieces, as the enormous humidity reduced me to a sort of hoarse liquid, how simply difficult it might be to store books in Nigeria. I had in mind all the time a library I'd seen, in which all the books had been dimmed to such a colour as suggested they'd been dipped in salt. They were the mouldiest possible ghosts of books. And gramophone records I'd seen in a broadcasting studio on Cape Coast. The air conditioning had failed for an hour or so, and now they had all these records, incredibly twisted ...

And at the end of that day, Harry had suggested the night club.

Immense noise, gloom, the milling figures of girls with wigs like busbies. We had with us a sharp-tongued young woman, Jane, a friend of Harry's, who seemed to have no patience with anyone. The whites who were present, she said, had contempt for the girls they came here to garner, and the blacks were interested only in self-satisfying sex, and they too cared nothing for the girls. I was simply astonished by the enormous noise, the dimness, the vigour of the band, the erotic character of the dancing. Harry and Joanna danced, and I half-heard what Jane was shouting: that too much sympathy should not be wasted on the Nigerians, they had had it altogether too easy. They had no social conscience, she yelled. 'Let them go through the hard things we went through in the West.' She'd come to Africa with high hopes, but her first experience had been of a massacre—of Ibos, in the north. The friends she was staying with had hidden an Ibo for two days. The whites had formed a police force. 'I didn't expect to be proud of being a European—I mean, it was the last thing I'd come to Africa for—but I *was*.'

She was clearly suffering from the most enormous shock of disenchantment, though the word was perhaps too easy: it must have been horrible, horrible. There was no arguing with it. And what to say, anyway—except what, against the background of that still sore experience, would have seemed ... either over-subtle or indifferent? It must have penetrated deeper than any level of debate, that experience of being a witness to the cruel murder of men and women from the east of the country: carried out up there in the north, where I'd just come from, in Kano and Zaria, by men with faces much like those of the young writers in my TV workshop.

Suddenly, in the deafening darkness of this night club, I was surrounded by voices full of hatred for Nigeria. There was a seaman sitting opposite, speaking of Nigerians as some special human dross: not, he said, ever to be trusted. 'Well,' I said, thinking of the titles of novels by Achebe—himself an Ibo, at this moment somewhere in Biafra—the phrases from Yeats that he'd used to sum up his accounts of the arrival in Nigeria of the white man: *No Longer at Ease, Things Fall Apart.* 'We did interfere,' I said. The seaman held his fists like a boxer's in front of his face. 'I don't like that word "interfere," ' he shouted.

I thought how I'd been advised in London to take care in mentioning Ibo writers, Achebe, Elechi Amadi, the poet Christopher Okigbo, and how I'd found that it clearly would have been thought odd to be silent about them. Well, on my arrival at the Airport Hotel, the first thing I'd seen was the receptionist, his nose in *Things Fall Apart,* so riveted by the work of the enemy that I had to wait for his attention.

Harry re-appeared, with a small slim girl he'd been dancing with. Christiana was certain Joanna would be angry when she got back from dancing herself—she'd be furious with Harry for having danced with Christiana at all, and worse for having brought her back to his table. And when Joanna appeared, and wasn't angry, she was astonished. Harry and I, she said candidly, were 'old pappas', not like the angry sailor, who was 'young man.' But for all my antiquity she took me away to dance with her, a sort of jigging up and down ...

It was when I walked among the tables in search of a lavatory that I experienced those graspings and animatory pressures I'd have been glad of a few evenings before, when my circulation failed in the garden of the British High Commission. Harry said he'd become shockingly ... he wouldn't say hardened ... accustomed to the experience himself, but it had made it impossible for him to take seriously such a phrase as 'running the gauntlet'.

165

6

I was a whole team of lecturers, now in the university, now (it seemed probable that these adverbs referred to the same moment) in schools, colleges, teachers' centres. I took part again in a television discussion, this time on African writing. I expressed my admiration for Amos Tutuola, whose Yoruba legends in marvellously strong broken English—language shattered to good purpose—are not updatings but extensions of a still-living line of stories. Ah, said a representative of the Ministry of Education, such rubbish, Tutuola's writings! In a language that nobody ever used! And in any case, hardly worth writing down, since you could hear such stuff any day in the nearest market!

But then, it was always difficult to talk of Tutuola, since it so easily appeared that he was being valued for something for which the horrible word might be 'quaintness'. What my admiration might seem to be saying was that I thought the best of Nigerian writing incapable of grammatical correctness.

I visited primary schools in Old Lagos. The apparent casual chaos of one with 2500 pupils in the morning, and another 1500 in the afternoon. Weaving crowds in brown uniforms in a great brown playground; many standing, lying, reading, playing games under an immense shade tree. It was the negation of respectable British order and surveillance, and I imagined the incredulity of old colleagues: myself warming to the sheer busy mystery of it. In another school, five classrooms in sequence, with half-walls, wildly battered desks, again the great noise and movement, with slow clouds of smoke, from some source that wasn't obvious, drifting from one shouting room to the next. And a third that was a dark barn, that had been made by cutting the top off a one-time

166

mosque; again, thunderous noise; a play being performed in Yoruba, with great energy and earnestness, by children perched on a stage made out of a great shaky stacking of desks. There in the darkness the actors made no effort to be heard above the roar of the audience, which in its turn made no obvious effort to listen, though there was all the same an effect of tumultuous attentiveness. At a desk of his own sat the teacher, at intervals ringing a bell: which produced no change of behaviour in any quarter.

Not, it must be said, that there was anywhere a feeling of indiscipline, in any sense familiar to me. It seemed simply ... mysterious and different.

I gave my lecture with its now familiar diffident title, 'A Distant View of African Literature', to an audience of, as it seemed, random diplomats and scholars. My chairman was the principal of the learned institute in which I was speaking. His vote of thanks turned out to be longer than my address—and, indeed, was a detailed critique of it. It was clear that I'd come through with colours that, if not flying, were decently flapping. I had been wrong at scores of points, but it had been right for me to be wrong.

We beamed, and I felt extraordinarily faint.

I was required to submit myself at once for interview on radio. Very well, said Harry, and drove to the studio with me in the official car. A sentry advanced towards us as we advanced towards him; he levelled an automatic weapon, making loud machine-gun noises as he did so. 'Back the car!' cried Harry. 'Back the car and let Edward proceed on foot!' The car was backed and, mildly incredulous, I walked towards the sentry, whose imitation of a gleeful executioner became even more exuberant. Somehow I found myself beyond him, unshot, and in the care of a producer. *He* had difficulty in persuading technicians to collaborate; we sat about helplessly, for a while, some obscure dispute lazily raging in the background. It came to an end; we made our recording; and I found myself, in that intoxicating darkness, again approaching the sentry box, though now from behind. This seemed an even worse relationship to the box than the one that had appalled me on arrival. I was not cheered when the producer disentangled himself precisely as Harry Lane had done the other way round. 'Just walk quietly towards him and stop when challenged,' he said. I had a sudden inconsequent memory of having been once a contributor to the BBC's Children's Hour. Then I was past the sentry box and had glimpsed, in that savoury dusk, the infinitely desirable official car, waiting, The sentry, I had made out, was fast asleep ...

7

Wole Soyinka, the Yoruba poet and playwright, has taken the road between Lagos and Ibadan as a symbol of life itself. This is because it was then certainly one of the most dangerous roads in the world. I was advised to consider prayer as a way of making the journey endurable. 'And on the whole,' someone added, 'keep the eyes shut.'

My driver made one comment only before we began: it was that he did not want to die. I was glad to find that this was his position, but as a statement by one's chauffeur, it did tighten the screw. We floated along in this very large car on this broken road in the foolhardy company of mammy trucks. There were tremendous hootings; at times, the car leapt into the air, thrown upwards by some amazing combination of ruts and craters. I tried not to read the feverish extracts from the Bible painted across the brows of the madly overtaking trucks, which seemed, being so overloaded, to be about to burst and scatter their passengers like the seed of one of those plants that propagate themselves by explosion. Every few yards along the side of the road there were the wrecked remains of vehicles. In that atmosphere they'd turned almost at once to shapes of rust, and were wrapped, sometimes quite beautifully, in leaf and flower. Floods had nibbled away at the already vague edges of the road: in places it was a ribbon, of a car's width only; in other places, no more than a sequence of deep holes, a kind of arterial doily. I felt a tiny

trembling literary satisfaction, being able to check on Soyinka's use of this highway as an image of mortal peril.

Ibadan itself was an immense confusion: as if the whole
world had gathered on this one spot to shout, laugh, and
bang tins together; being hugged, throughout the performance, by flames. It was enormously hot in this city that,
from any distance, was a great lake of rusty roofs. We entered
it through a hubbub of tiny workshops and rickety offices,
proclaiming themselves the Go-Ahead Institute for Steno-
graphers, the Beat-the World College of Typewriting, the
Best-of-all Bookshop, and so on. One of the tiniest of the
workshops, a kind of roofed crate, shouted out that it was
Doctor for Volkswagens.

And the next day we pressed on, following a road that was
being remade, though there was never a sign of work in
progress. One could say only that the road had been gathered
at some time into heaps and moved vaguely in new directions, leaving canyons, composed of the most outrageously red
dust, for us to drive through. It was a brilliant, mysterious
wound deep in the green world of the forest. At times we had
to guess at our own existence somewhere inside swelling and
tottering clouds of dust. We were alone inside these huge
billowings, a succession of silent explosions of redness, and the
only other colour in the world was the luminous green of the
trees. If the day before's had been the most dangerous, this
was the most brilliant journey I'd known.

I was to talk at a teachers' training college: my subject, as
set down in the programme of my grandly named Tour of the
Western State, being: 'The Literate Teacher: The Teacher's
Role in the Encouragement of Reading.' I felt by now like
one of the local lizards: orange creatures, given to sudden
diagonal presence and sudden diagonal absence, their lives
entirely devoted to being alarmed. My thoughts, at any rate,
were becoming lizardy: they flickered in and out of the
foliage of my mind. Good Lord, yes, I was becoming inwardly
a forest. Africa had begun to grow inside me.

I was dismayed by the way my audience was dressed—the
men being in suits, the girls in blouses and skirts. Europe had
laid its hands on the college and banished colour. The girls
had none of the straight-up-and-downness that made sense of
tailored skirts. Was it really believed that sombre and alien

169

formality was an essential ingredient in the make-up of a teacher?

The vice-principal was English: the principal a Nigerian. The first appeared; the second didn't. This, I was told, was because of his very great shyness. He didn't come to a party given for me that evening. But next morning, very early, I was summoned: I was to go across to his house. He had become bold, at last. I sat in his austere study, lined with Loeb editions of the Latin authors—he was a classical scholar—and drank brandy. It was seven o'clock of an already hot African morning, and I had had no breakfast. Here, in the company of this charming shy man, who smiled more than he conversed—and was, I believe, unconvinced that an African might be principal and a European only his deputy—I was drinking breathtaking spirits, and feeling more lizardy than ever.

8

'Stop,' said Akin. We got out of the car: Robert, my friend from East Africa, a couple of literary academics, one Ghanaian, one from Sierra Leone; a young Nigerian poet; and Akin himself, a student at the University of Ife, who'd arranged this appointment with palm wine in the local forest.

Under moonlight, blanched paths wound through gently creaking shadow. I realised that all forests, English, Greek, African, were more alike than I'd ever imagined. We came to a glade; and there the palm wine was waiting for us, stored in a low thatched shelter. It was of the appearance, and even more of the taste, of soapy water, but it had, in reserve, quite unsoapy qualities. Detonations in the nostrils; the sinuses filled with deliciously displeasing fumes. One's head taken over by foreign delights.

There was a trick, when it came to the last drops in a

calabash. You threw them, with a quick jerk of the wrist, to the ground; where, if it was properly done, they exploded. There was a positive small bang. I think I was successful with my first attempt at this. But I am certain of nothing that happened. A reeling vagueness occurred early on. I remember a singing voice, and a lantern, and then the wine tapster himself appearing, with more wine, and fiercely baked fragments of chicken for us to break our teeth on.

What I do certainly recall is my sudden patriotism. I could not, I declared, understand their passion for Africa, if I had no similar passion for England, and made much of this; they responding with speeches of their own and sympathetic minglings of belch and sigh. I'd been moved to it by the loveliness of this setting, and by the way it reminded me of our woods at home.

I have also a fair recollection of having proposed all sorts of loyal toasts, of a literary nature.

I was in Ife for a conference on African writing in English—the last engagement of my tour. So obviously absent that it hurt were the Nigerians, Achebe and Ekwensi, in Biafra, and Wole Soyinka, imprisoned for finding the war absurd. Absent, indeed, were all creative writers except the novelists Ngugi and Rubadiri from East Africa. Present were representatives of a new generation of African critics, one of whom spoke, for them all, of the need 'to see African literature in its African essence', and to travel beyond pleasure in the mere existence of African writing in English to the establishment of strict standards of judgement.

Africa, I thought, was beginning to take its own literature into its own critical hands. Hurrah! Other presences came from European and American universities; and some, it was difficult not to feel, represented academic empires, which happened to rest on the existence of African literature. I felt the non-African academic presence here as a sort of brittleness. It had a busy, clacking voice. The African voice in the conference was quite different. Rubadiri's, for example, talking about the way in which the colonial experience in East Africa had been such as to stifle every attempt to use the acquired language; to ensure that there was no local publishing; to make it seem necessary to 'please teacher.' For a long time, said Rubadiri, no one had reached back, as writers had done in West Africa, to the traditional culture. It had been with feverish excitement (it was his phrase) that across *there* they'd realised that over *here* writers had begun to write about Africa in a wholly African fashion.

I thought there was a new confidence, among all these presences and absences; and it lay in the discovery that the old oral traditions provided a voice for the African writer even when, using a language that wasn't African, he treated of themes that weren't old. There was a belief now in a deeply African writing, surrounded by thoroughly African criticism.

I talked of my outsider's problems. That one simply of deciding what the judgement should be if a young poet used a word that, through over-use or because it has passed into the vocabulary of the poetaster, had become in a purely English context unuseable. 'Take the word "sublime", which it is very difficult for an English writer to use now, either in poetry or in prose. The English ear may reject it because, in the nature of things, the English ear is sensitive to the nuances of English vocabulary, within an absolutely English context. But to an African poet, against a background in which there may have been so much misuse of a word, any term so dead to an English ear may to his own ear still be vibrant with its original life. Is there to be a general rule that the African writer using English must be governed by English experience of the language? Or is he free to start afresh?'

Inevitable that, for some time to come, critics of African writing in English would find themselves preoccupied with questions of this nature. 'But while the critics worry about them, as they must, the creative writers drive ahead, as *they* must, erecting their own rules. I do not believe that African poets, novelists, playwrights, are going to be content with correct usage, as the schoolmaster (as *he* must, perhaps) measures correctness. I fully understand that for many African writers using English, the dread of being valued outside Africa for mere quaintness is very strong. I am worried, I must say, from time to time because some of my African friends suspect that my admiration for the writing of Amos Tutuola—'

('I knew you'd talk about Tutuola!' Jenny Mallet would say, back in London)

'—is founded on improper grounds: they believe that I find

172

Tutuola's English "picturesque", and that my enjoyment of it is in some way patronising. This, when the charge is made, I can only vigorously deny. No Englishman with any ear has difficulty in understanding Amos Tutuola: that is to say, he doesn't begin to be unintelligible. Far from it. The breaches of correct usage, the unfinished sentences, the idiosyncratic use of relative pronouns, and so on, form no bar to understanding; at the same time, echoing as they do the vernacular usage, they create *an African voice in English* that makes an English reader feel he has come closer to the tone of Yoruba storytelling than he could easily have done had the language been more conventional. And all that apart, Tutuola handles language like a poet: there is that constant liveliness and alertness in the choice and disposition of words that is the mark of the true writer.'

Oh yes—the African writer using English would surely, very soon, by the sheer force of his creative concentration on his task, carry us beyond such dilemmas of judgement.

And I tried to sum up my outsider-insider's feeling—more difficult than ever, in the midst of this indubitable Africa, where every night I slept my hot wet sleep as if it were something I'd been nailed up in ... my feeling about the task of the African writer. 'You have to create a new literature in the shadow of a very old and very assured achievement in the same basic tongue. At the same time, you have to do this under the eye of the schoolmaster and the critic. To me, the birth of African writing in English is like nothing so much as the outburst of modern English literature in the Elizabethan period. Suppose the Elizabethans had been subject to the same intricate and massive critical and pedagogical apparatus to which you are subject? What would Shakespeare have done with the *Times Literary Supplement, Encounter,* the University Departments of English looking over his shoulder? But whenever I think of this sort of thing, of all this range of questionings and nigglings that gather round African writing in English, I then think of the power of the creative spirit itself, as well as of a great deal that has actually been achieved: and I know that in ten years most of these elementary puzzlings and ponderings will have been swept away.'

And the help that was being offered by non-African

radio—like my own programme? I was awfully aware of the limitations of what it could do. It could encourage, and give a hearing, and offer a limited amount of advice. But the best it could do might not be enough to keep a young writer of promise afloat.

'Perhaps at this stage there might be some safety net, some body of African writers to whom young people, or apprentice writers of any age, might be referred? This may be difficult to bring about—but I worry a good deal about the fate, as writers, of some promising contributors to the programme.'

A year or so later, when the whole of this strange experience blew up in my face—the planters of the bomb claiming that I was a Western flatterer of African writers who'd been turned into bogus Westerners themselves—I thought back to this paper given at Ife. Applying all sorts of fairly obvious tests for flattery—fawning language, caressive quality of judgement, a certain arrangement of the knees—I found it difficult to condemn myself along those lines.

Self-condemnation I did frame, indeed, when the time came: but on very different grounds.

9

If I think back to Nigeria, it is often the main street in Ife that I see. Everywhere that ruddiness of earth and walls and roofs. The tumbled brilliant interiors of shops—some of them standing on thick platforms of earth. The sense of so much that's on the move—not only men and women and children, but goats and chickens—and, a special sort of Nigerian animal, cyclists. A thick flow of living things, all shouting, bleating or clucking at the tops of their voices. Somehow, in the middle of it, there's my absurd official car, brimming with Africans who are wearing their learning not so much

174

lightly as hilariously. Michael, the chauffeur, sits haughtily at the wheel. He does not like these academics and students, he is distressed by their addiction to the Inferno, the night club where we end so many evenings, awash with that beer that I continue to find unsatisfactory. Michael's objection to the Inferno is expressed always in the same phrases: 'Bad place— no latrines.' After sundown he changes his neat suit for robes, but this does not make him feel more kindly towards the Inferno. It is also possible to feel that he does not enjoy exposing the car to what can't quite be called traffic jams—they are simply voluntary coagulations of assorted creatures and conveyances. He is particularly horrified when a drunken soldier hammers on the boot with a bottle, demanding that we open up and let him get at us. What he wants to do with us is uncertain—but clearly the bottle would play a part in it. He dabs with it at the windows; Michael accelerates and a huge section of the crowd takes to its heels, hoofs and wings.

I now hate, in addition to buffet suppers and the local beer, all air conditioning; my suitcases; and every item of my clothing. My contempt for my underwear is rivalled only by my detestation of my shirts.

It is the final confusion of the tour: studded with marvels. Such as the evening when we watch a Nigerian version of the story of Oedipus. Not that it's a mere adaptation of a Greek original. I was taken the next morning to the crossroads, not far from the town, where the Oedipus-figure met and slew his father. It was a local tale, and the Greeks need not have bothered. It also had a quality that pre-dated the division of drama into comedy and tragedy. Up to the very last awful moment, Oedipus was weeping with amusement as readily as he wept with despair. Jokes kept pace with terrible revelations. There were marvellous moments in the staging—as when a whole army came sweeping through the audience to attack the palace. They caused delighted dismay to great numbers of small children—some extremely small—who throughout the evening had shuffled on their bottoms closer and closer to the stage, until in the end they were gazing up at the actors, a frieze of gawpers. It went on till one o'clock in the morning, when it seemed unlikely that I could be— though I so patently *was*—awake.

And other moments that seemed unlikely: as when Akin

took me to his home village, a few miles from the town, and introduced me to the priest who'd watched over his progress from school to university. We walked down the village street, Akin throwing himself forward on his hands as he encountered relatives, and exchanging the quick intricate patter of formal greeting; and then, there was the new church the priest was building, as large as one of the great East Anglian churches in the richest centres of the wool trade. I said thoughtlessly that it would be difficult in Britain now to fill a church half as large, and the priest was saddened. 'We have this image of England ...' he said.

I sat watching films. The head of a goat was sawn through, and the headless body kicked hideously. I'd read with ease, in African stories, so many accounts of sacrifices, the beheading of goats and chickens. What you could endure bravely in words, you flinched from when it was to be seen. There was a film of women dancing. In one long sequence they were down on their haunches, clasping each other's waists, and the dance, a response to the urgent repetitions of drums, was a long sway and stir of the single creature they composed. I thought it was the most beautiful dancing I'd ever seen: prepared to perfection, yet achieving what seemed worlds away from anything like rehearsal or drill.

I was becoming squeamish, alas, nothing but Nigerian food now being available: it was like eating rainbows, such colours! But I hadn't adjusted to it. Robert ate ochra soup with his fingers, long sticky bright green strings of it hanging from finger tips and mouth. He even made gestures with it. My appetite grew smaller still.

And the conference continued, given to that absurd habit of having contributors speak from papers already cyclostyled and distributed. It could most easily become a way of not listening to what one had not read. Several had that approach to literature that made them, I'd think, the work of Professors of Blurb-Writing. But dullness was not quite dishonourable: negligence was. One paper promising a grand view of African writing dwindled to a discussion of a few recent novels. I'd read them all, and was shocked to hear their stories being inaccurately summarised by a speaker who was appallingly confident in his mispronunciation of the names of authors and characters.

176

Small wonder that James Ngugi, the only major writer present, was exasperated by conferences and academics. He talked with brief intensity of the failure of the African writer to deal with the present. Everywhere, after independence, the writer had been 'merely a liberal referee'. He ought to be committed, and to take the side of the majority 'whose silent clamour for change,' said Ngugi, was 'now rocking the continent.'

It was the expression of impatience from an obvious viewpoint. It was deeply-felt, convinced and angry. If it was a cue for discussion—and it was probably much more concerned with the need to write than with any need to talk about writing—then it pointed to some other gathering than this, infinitely less tidy and infinitely more passionate.

I thought how odd it was, this encounter of academics and writers in the setting of this campus, where university buildings had barely yet imposed their spirit on the site. It seemed a sort of wilderness, still, these hills, patches of forest, shrieking with birds.

The academic certainly had a gift for reducing texts to unexcitement. He had this knack of turning the liveliest material into laundry lists. There were exceptions: my friend Robert, agonisedly involved with Africa, was one. But I was so often reminded of an occasion when I'd stood with Ngugi in a university bookshop, and he'd come across a book offering students advice on how to answer questions about one of his novels. He was astonished: barely recognised the author under discussion, was wholly unfamiliar with this particular specimen of the man's work ...

The drumming as the dancers swayed, swung, turned their heads this way and that ... Oh, but the academic certainly had ways of muffling the drums!

In the early morning, women carrying water: on each head, half a dozen gourds on a round wooden tray. Something else I'd read about, again and again: but how beautiful it was, seen! I ought to be thinking, of course, about the abominable labour required of women. Well, I *was* thinking of it! But how very lovely they looked, in that early light, as we drove past in our fat car, product of a fat other world. Arranged in order of height, and singing! And not one of them in starched blouse or tailored skirt!

And after them, a whole village coming down a hill from church, compensating for any anaemia in their dress by carrying multi-coloured umbrellas ...

Lagos-Ibadan in reverse. It was a Moslem holiday: the newspapers foresaw a weekend of disaster. 'Safe journey!' everyone said: but it was a local phrase dating from before the motorcar.

Leaving Ibadan, Michael added us to other vehicles in the ditch. We'd encountered the military governor. Police car with screaming siren; armoured car with grim-faced sten-gunner sprawled on the roof; outriders on motorcycles; governor's car. When it was possible again to hear the normal din of the town, we crept back on the road. Michael sat stiff and silent for half an hour, to make up for the indignity of it.

He also jumped the queues at Army check-points, having a way of sliding and slinking forward that gave to this large car the attributes of a cunning schoolboy.

And Lagos again! All the scenes I'd longed to have means of fixing in my memory. The Night Time Hotel—a terracotta smoothing-iron of a building, each room in its three storeys being a simple box with garishly painted door; many doors always open, so that the interiors of the rooms looked like tiny theatres; the balconies garish, too, with cloths spread out to dry. And one whole area of the city, an open space that was, in effect, a huge laundry, a mass of cloths laid out, of every colour. The rainbow again, chopped up and the fragments shuffled and laid end to end. Every inch of the city was remarkable. The Carter Bridge, its parapets being friezes of moving heads, on every head a burden: from the simplest, a sack or two, to mounds of furniture, complex machines, towers of paper. And round the roots of the bridge, on each shore, entire colonies in shacks, every square yard a complex city of its own.

Do Not, the walls cried, Urinate Here. And whenever the moving congestion of things became a halted congestion, still there were so many elements in this city that never stood still, like the armless and legless man whose remnants, mounted on a pair of planks with wheels, whipped carelessly across the street, defying the dangerous impatience of cars, lorries, buses, hand-drawn carts.

And the number of the legless and armless was growing

178

every day. Those mutilated soldiers I'd seen being lifted in and out of aeroplanes ...

We arrived late at Harry Lane's house in Ikoyi. The boundary hedge was the haunt of the local prostitute, who stepped out now into the light of the car and smiled, with an effect of unusual official welcome. I tried to imagine such lively use being made of stretches of well-to-do privet, back at home.

Where Kate was waiting for me, quite as if, a month before, I'd let go her arm in some fairground and gone into a sideshow; and there she was, patient, in the same place; and I'd had this improbable experience, and didn't know how I'd ever tell her about it.

PART FIVE

1

'Ted complains,' wrote my father in his oblique way, 'about the climate of Nigeria. We could have told him it would not suit him. His chest has never been very strong and, of course, he doesn't lead as active a life as some. Many people keep fit by gardening, but he has never found much time for this. We have several neighbours who are finding it difficult to keep going because they have sat on their b-t-m's all their lives. We wonder if Catherine is wise not to see that Ted gets out and about a bit more.'

It was designed to cause as much irritation as possible. I had described the problems of carrying out a long programme while still adjusting to the immense humidity of a country like Nigeria, but this was a descriptive item in the letter I'd written, and in no way a complaint. I was considerably more active than many of my literary friends: walked, for example, perhaps a hundred times further a year than Rufus, who seemed to believe that even moderate use of the legs might be destructive to the literary gift. He would always expect writer's cramp to attack the knee. The implication in my father's reference to Kate was that she was a fool, and a negligent fool at that. The letter was the most negative possible response to my account of my journey.

The fact was, however, that I was in favour. It had not, for years, been possible for my sister and me to be in his good books at the same time. She was enormously out of them, at the moment. Or rather, her husband was out of them, and had taken her with him—he being held bitterly to have added to that original crime of his, of having married her. He had, for example, obliged her to live in a suburb of London so low-lying that they and their children were constantly subject to colds. My father had never had any doubt that colds were

183

caused by altitude, or rather by its absence. 'Damned silly place to live.' He had made various domestic purchases that my father regarded as acts of insanity. Why *this* when he hadn't got *that?* 'We wonder sometimes how his mind works.' An expert on insurance, Brian had offered my father some perfectly ordinary, sensible advice. Bloody cheek! 'And you wouldn't find there was nothing in it for Brian! You can bet your life on that!'

About my sister's marriage, as about mine, my father took it for granted that we had fallen into the hands of monstrous persons, and were trying to conceal the misery we felt. But he was not deceived! Oh no! And there was this matter of Brian having allowed oil to leak out of his car onto the floor of my father's garage. This was an act of negligence, laced with malice, that had made it impossible to maintain the garage in the only condition which my father thought suitable for it: that of immaculacy and general perfection.

And Betty had gone on a visit, hoping to put things straight; and it had resulted in things being put rather more crooked than before. Just as he had thought fit from time to time to entertain me with his view of Kate's father ('We're not impressed by Brown's pose of being poor—you usually find that sort of person has a fortune tucked away'), so he attacked Brian's father ('Not a ha'porth of brains'). Betty, who'd started out with the hope we always had, of a pleasant visit, was close to tears. Then he said, harshly: 'I wanted to talk to you about something. It's about my funeral.' It was a matter of who should be there—or rather, who should *not*. No relatives. He didn't want his brother George, or his brother Will. In fact, no one was to be told of it till it was safely over. He didn't want anyone pretending to cry over his going.

As Betty said ruefully, going on a visit when he was in this mood was like attempting some very difficult embassage. It would make it so much easier if you could begin with an offer of gifts, in the historically favoured line of gold, silver and precious gems.

2

There came now the last of those occasions when my father was taken by surprise ... by happiness. Oddly enough, it was a family occasion. A nephew was to be married, at some distance from New Chilton. Kate and I arranged to be my parents' chauffeurs.

It wasn't likely to resemble the last family wedding Kate and I had attended—involving a cousin from what might be described as the intellectual end of the family spectrum. Present were representatives of the other—the aggressively thoughtless—end. They circulated, these cousins, among the astonished guests, spreading a certain view of human difference. There were, they festively held, those whose energy was in their heads; and those whose energy was in their loins. They themselves, my cousins, were clear that they had the secret of the latter, and infinitely preferable, type of energy. As the wedding feast took hold of their spirits, they offered themselves as consolations to the bride, to Kate, and to the wife (three thousand miles absent, but no matter) of a cousin who was a North American academic. I was reminded of my family's explosive sensuality and its objection to anything that replaced carnal triumph with any other sort of achievement.

This wedding promised to be very different: innocent, rural. It involved a trip across country, a night in a hotel.

Hardness of hearing now shut my mother away from the world much of the time, she had an imprisoned look; but on this occasion, breaking through those deaf walls, I found that, inside, she was fairly capering with delight. It was the first time for a long while that they'd left the bungalow. All her pleas for adventurous weekends ten miles or so along the coast had fallen on. ears, my father's, that were deafer than her own. The bungalow was a fortress from which they must

185

emerge only for the most remarkable reasons. This, then, was her first opportunity to wear various items of finery acquired for phantom excursions, holidays that never were. She rather overdid it, draping herself in contradictory novelties of costume.

There was a blue turban that was lushly out of sympathy with her tiny, wrinkled, sensible face. There was also a surprisingly transparent dress that turned out to have a story behind it. She'd bought it, she told me, in revenge for an incident more than fifty years old. My father had proposed to her at some point during the First World War, sitting on a stile in the middle of what is now a congested London suburb. They'd gone at once to my father's home, told my grandmother and shown her the ring. Annie had been wearing a fine blouse, charcoal grey and white, with a bodice extremely visible underneath it, through the neck of which this most undesigning of girls had threaded, with a loving wickedness entirely directed at my father, a pink ribbon. The response to the news of the engagement by my grandmother, most designing of women, was to call my father out of the room and urge that his fiancée (as she supposed she must call her) was immodestly dressed ...

My father loved the journey. He was delighted to lunch in a country pub. He praised Kate's driving. When she stopped to allow him a long stare at a house he admired, he was overwhelmed by the courtesy of it. 'That was very thoughtful of you, Catherine,' he said, and it was almost as if he'd called her Kate. He liked the hotel, a place as dilapidated as it was large: its rooms vast, filled with ill-matched mammoths of furniture. Rather grand, he thought. He was deeply pleased by our all being together for dinner—my sister and her husband having joined us. He called for wine with none of his usual ironies and innuendos, and insisted that one bottle should be dry, for our sakes. 'Well, it's a matter of taste,' he explained, largely. 'If I drank enough, I suppose I might like it dry, too.' His laugh was designed to correct a little the amiable implications of this remark. But his good humour in general was, to Kate and me, the best of intoxicants. We waltzed along absurd corridors to our absurd bed.

And in the morning I went in to see how they'd slept, and my mother was a tiny staring figure, in huge white bloomers, looking like some Spanish grandee, remarkably shrivelled but still authoritative. 'We slept like—', she said, and then couldn't remember what you slept like. 'We had a good night's sleep.'

Two of my father's brothers were at the wedding. There was Uncle Will, who'd always seemed jolly—but rather mockingly so: there'd been a period during my childhood when, to add strength to some point of view or other, he'd written to my father on lavatory paper. He was, I suppose, the grey sheep of the family. He greeted me teasingly now, and I suddenly felt small, remembering exactly how his approaches had filled me with apprehensive affection. I recalled his crowning a story long ago by turning to me: 'Don't *you* be a muggins, Teddy!' Then, to my father: 'You're not going to let this lad grow up into a muggins, are you, Dick?' It was a question to which I'd have liked to hear an answer. Was I to be permitted or encouraged to grow up into a muggins? It seemed a plausible destiny. But I'd detected a wink travelling between uncle and father. They were having me on. Or Uncle Will was having me on, and my father was allowing it ...

There was also Uncle Arthur, always the most excitable of the brothers: an over-lively young face having become simply an over-lively old one. The uncles set on my father together, exploring the joke of his having been a civil servant. 'Not wearing your medals, Dick?' roared Uncle Will. It was an inquiry that might have resulted in chairs flying about the room, fifty years earlier. It was followed by reference to his MBE, which made my father quiver with anger. Well, he *had* made an awful lot of that mechanical honour, quite apart from hanging the citation in the hall at home, in New Chilton. It was what almost certainly had led, one or two Christmases earlier, to the arrival of a card from a neighbour, addressed to 'Sir Richard and Lady Blishen, OBE.' My father, before severing diplomatic relations—except that with him it would have been undiplomatic relations he'd severed —asked me if I thought it was meant as a joke. I think he was genuinely reluctant to conclude that such a subject could be regarded as fit matter for levity.

There was now, at my father's expense, an outburst of jibes. The whole of their childhood was in Uncle Will's allegation that someone had spilled grapefruit—something spitty, fizzy, disgusting—on the back of my father's jacket. How well he knew what would disturb that immaculate man! It was rain, said my father—it had been a wet day, off and on. No more than rain! Rain! jeered Uncle Will. The colour mounted in my father's face. My mother was no help at all, having long ago divided her love between all the brothers. They were so alike, to look at: I think she'd truly felt, when she made their acquaintance sixty years earlier in the slums of Edwardian London, that they were variations on a single physically desirable theme. She was coquettish in their presence, as though still free to choose among them. It was Kate who had to assure my father that there was nothing on the back of his jacket, at all.

It was the last time these men met. They parted, displeased or mocking as they'd always been. I'd loved my uncles, forty years before, for the very mischief that lay behind so much of their behaviour to each other. I saw now that ever since their rough-edged childhood they'd been rivals—to the death. Any one of them might do anything to another, if a kind of cruel fun might be the result. Well, there was that story I'd heard from my mother, who'd heard it from my father, of their discovery that their parents made love regularly after Sunday dinner, in a bedroom of which the door was never completely shut. So they made a little breathless queue, taking turns to stare through the crack of the door, until one who was at the end—and it might have been any of them—gave a sudden push, and they all tumbled, calamitously, into the passionate room ...

3

There'd been talk off and on, as long as I could remember, of the Millers, with whom my mother and father had shared a house in the 1920s, early in the marriages of both couples. The men had been in the Army together, and they'd had a decisive effect on each other's lives. My father had come home, wounded—there was a vacancy for a clerk in the War Office, and Miller somehow had the disposing of it: which was how my father and the Civil Service came together. Later in his turn he suggested Miller when another job was offered. And that led, for a while, to this sharing of a rented house. The memories were all of marvellously lively evenings: singing at the piano; Mrs Miller's affection for my mother; and the pleasure she took in me, as a baby. I'd loved hearing, when I was young, references to the Millers: they sounded so happy, jolly. I imagined them, all four, young and sparkling, standing round a candle-lit piano. Much laughter, and teasing. Somewhere in a corner of the scene, harder to imagine, myself, rather wasting the opportunity; that is, in no position to take notes.

And I'd found that Mrs Miller was still alive, a widow, in her eighties; and she lived near the route we must take when we returned to New Chilton. So it was arranged that we'd call. It would be a curious and moving coda to the outing.

We let my mother and father go in first, expecting the reunion to be rather much for them all. But this little, bent, bright-eyed woman barely had eyes for them. To Kate she said, referring to me: 'May I kiss this man—he was my first baby!' I was kissed, and we took up positions that never varied throughout the visit. Mrs Miller with Kate, of whom she'd made instantly her prime audience, fixing her with the shining eyes of someone accustomed to conquest. Kate was to be made her slave, her faithful listener. I saw how she must have enslaved my very enslaveable mother, all those years before. 'My dear little Annie!' she cried now—how she made not only slaves but pets of people!—but went on at once to something else, and my mother looked baffled and irritable. She and my father sat in the background throughout the visit, tired and deeply puzzled, barely speaking, barely spoken to.

It was a confused and confusing house. Everywhere clippings from newspapers, photographs, tumbling heaps of magazines. On a table were sandwiches Mrs Miller said she'd prepared the day before: they were shrouded in a teacloth, and were inevitably dry and inedible. She began at once a long monologue. It was an extraordinary performance. I thought at first she was spilling her memories with the freedom of someone shaking apples out of a tree; but then I

189

saw that her talk, this candid flow, was made up of many evasions. She was talking so freely in order not to talk about matters concerning which my father had a blunt curiosity. About, for example, Miller's career after they'd lost sight of one another in the late 1920s. How he'd died. The truth about some miserable affair in Miller's official life, when he'd been held responsible for an error that had led to someone's death. Mrs Miller, I'm sure, heard these questions being asked—or attempts being made at the asking of them—and understood the straightforward nature of my father's interest, how for years he'd wanted to know about these things: but never meant to answer them.

She told the story of her meeting with Miller. In 1915 he'd been one of several soldiers billeted in the seaside house where she lived with her mother, a doctor's widow. From her bedroom she'd listened to them shaving and showering in the kitchen below—it was music in her ears; and as the old woman said so, the young woman's excitement spoke again. The sound of them shaving, washing, laughing, down below! Her whole story was punctuated with thrilled cries, expressions of wonder, that had nothing retrospective about them. It was as if, once this self-centred vivacity of hers had given rise to a response—any gasp, any cry—that response could be recalled and repeated for ever without loss of freshness.

Later Miller was in camp in the Midlands, and she wrote and asked him to meet her train as she made her way to stay with a friend in the North: but that was only a story, only a story! She'd never meant to continue the journey! There he was on the platform, and slowly, teasingly—she reproduced now the exact slow teasingness of it—she'd made it clear that she'd stay the whole day, the night, a whole week, if he would say the word. And (mesmerised, I guess) he said this amazed word, and she stayed. And wasn't nice to him. Oh, no: she spoke to him often with bitterness! Because, as she told him at last, she was twenty-nine. She had a possible career ahead of her, as a teacher. She had many qualifications! She could be a teacher most beautifully, in schools with fine names. She recited some of the names, with a little thrilled cry at each of them. But she wanted to marry, and had resolved that if she couldn't marry him, she would marry no one. Well, there it was: it was him, or nobody! So what would he say? And she was not nice to him, demanding a decision, sitting in a park in that garrison town: she was bitter and peremptory! And he said it was impossible, there was such a social gulf between them! Well, he was a Cockney, and she was refined, a doctor's daughter, and so on. And then suddenly, as if one half of him had spoken and had then conceded the day to a perfectly different half, he'd seized a finger, and put a ring on it—here it was, now, on her finger still! Well, yes, he'd been engaged, but it was to some barmaid, some coarse creature!

She talked on and on, her life now, her life then, all bound together in the same exclamatory freshness and thrilled intensity. My mother and father, looking very tired and frail, sat in bewildered silence; her back was to them, as she rambled on for Kate's sake; and Kate, mesmerised, began herself to purr and exclaim. And flies hovered over the dehydrated sandwiches, and my mother spent her time flapping at them, and staring incredulously at food so ineptly prepared, and at the cups of tea none of us drank, which had come out of the pot in which, under orders, I'd placed six exhausted tea bags.

And when we were going, the intensified brightening of the bright eyes, and the cry of: 'My dear little Annie!' My father's stumbling farewell, none of his questions answered. And in the car he spoke with astonishment of the relationship as it had really been ... as he now remembered it had really been. The terrible stresses that arose between the couples, partly because Miller was a man of great violence. Part of his violence must have sprung from his having made this marriage against his instinct. There'd been this girl from another social world who wanted him, and he'd been flattered and hated himself for being flattered, and she'd loved him for his physical strength and yet he'd been the most helpless victim when she bound him with her thrilling cries and the brightness with which she looked at him. The girl he'd been engaged to, my father remembered, wasn't coarse at all, wasn't even a barmaid—a nice, simple, jolly girl. Well, Miller had these fits of violence; my father had once thrown a chair at him, to keep him at bay. And it had never been comfortable when Miller's parents came to visit, very Cockney, his father cloth-capped. She'd not cared for them, at all. Nor had it been all happiness between the women. Oh,

191

far from it. My mother had been expected to provide all the practical domesticities. And Mrs Miller had objected to her feeding me when the Millers were present. Had been adamant about that: no breast-feeding while they were there.

Yet, said my father, there really were good times, when they sang songs, Mrs Miller at the piano.

'You must think,' he said wryly, 'that we've been inconsistent, in some of our stories.'

No, I said: of course, one could have superficial memories of people, and express and half-believe them, and over many years perhaps grow to believe them altogether, and then suddenly one could be reminded of the much less simple reality, and be shocked and shaken by the reminder.

And I thought how extraordinary it was, at this point in my relationship with my father, that we were discussing something that lay at the heart of our own misunderstandings: that matter of the possible truth of things against the certain untruth of things. Tired, still possessed by the pleasure of our excursion, my father was closer now than he'd ever been to offering straightforward companionship, the essence of it being the puzzled and pitying discussion of a human story.

Back in New Chilton he went at once to bed, and was there still when we left the next morning. He lay, when I went in to say goodbye, with his eyes closed: and very slowly, at the sound of my entry, he opened his eyes and said, 'I am so scared!'

I smiled, murmured reassurances, pressed his hand. He spoke again, with a sort of wonder, about how he'd enjoyed the outing, and the pubs we'd gone to, and how grateful he was to us, for being ferrymen. And he fumbled under the pillow and produced a five-pound note: it was for us to spend on lunch, on the way home.

And I wish things between us had ended then.

4

Jenny Mallet, I slowly realised, was uncomfortable about
something. Well, it seemed to be about this prestigious
African literary magazine, *Turningpoint*. I'd once said that I
thought it inappropriate, glossily grand, when what Africa
seemed to need was as many simple, accessible forms of
publishing as possible. Cyclostyled sheets. That was when my
meetings with young writers in Kampala, Kano, Zaria were
fresh in my mind. But I was perhaps wrong about it. Perhaps
in the world into which Africa had been dragged, it was
necessary in every field to show that one could be as splendid
as the rest.

The fact was that something clearly had been said in this
journal that was capable of giving me distress. I couldn't
imagine what it was; and no copy seemed to be available, in
any of the places where I might have expected to find it.

My African trips had certainly changed my understanding
of African texts in a multitude of tiny ways, as well as in one
or two large ways that I couldn't yet analyse. Some of these
changes were obvious, of course. When a poet contributed to
the programme a curiously eighteenth-century poem about
the Nigerian climate and wrote of the harmattan as

> Wind that comes cutting with chill incision
> Parching with utmost precision,

I was now able to colour these grey lines with a memory of
Kano on the night of my arrival. And when I read of palm
wine, I tasted it.

I was, oddly, both more and less certain about Africa than I
had been.

Still many stories that came in to the programme were

193

essentially … the sort of story a policeman tells in a witness box. Event flatly followed event. I wondered, having now heard so many vivacious tales from African mouths, how the knack of it, so obvious in speaking, vanished in writing. 'Having a story to tell,' I urged in what was to be one of the last of the programmes (for it had been decided that they'd had their day), 'one says: "You'll never guess who I met a moment ago"; and then "You'll never guess what he said to me." Certainly this *can* be irritating—when, for instance, the thing to be guessed at turns out to have been hardly worth all the mystery: but all the same, in everyday habits like this one we sometimes show a better instinct for storytelling than we do when we sit down with pen and paper.'

And a story so often thinned to a trickle, as the end neared, and then dried up, leaving a dismal moral sandbank. 'In life, the moral fact is rarely found pure: it's mixed up with other things: it's richly, and in a complex way, part of the texture of life, in which are found other strands than those of morality … The pure moral observation hardly covers all the quality of any human experience whatever.'

Jenny said that Prem, the editor of *Turningpoint,* was coming to London and wanted to interview me. He wanted to do the interviewing, she repeated anxiously. But he shouldn't do that, if I didn't like the idea.

Well, I said, I gathered he had some grudge against me, and I'd be glad to answer that, whatever it turned out to be. So she'd arrange it, would she? She gave me a tender, bothered answer. But then Jenny was tender and bothered about all her friends, having a general view of them as persons unfit to leave the security of their homes unaccompanied. I thought busily that it was a matter of her worrying about some edge of disagreeableness there might be to the interview.

I was wrong about that. Jenny had the measure of what was to happen.

When Prem arrived in the studio I offered my hand, saying 'Hallo.' He said, 'My God, here's the man who thinks he's perfect.' It seemed an odd description. 'What's behind that?' I asked. But he was saying that this was to be a great and rather terrifying interview, and that people should be summoned from all parts of the building to see him conduct it.

194

And what would we talk about? I asked. My God, he said, suddenly enormously ill-intentioned.

The green light went on, but I saw that it ought probably to have been a red one.

It was a rare pleasure to be in the presence of such an expert on African literature, he began. He himself, of course, only *lived* in Africa. First question: Why did I concern myself with African literature?

Because I liked it.

Why did I like it?

I was a writer, and interested in all writing.

Oh, was I? And in *(enormous, near-triumphant emphasis)* children's writing?

Yes.

Did I *(triumph on the verge of completion)* think Africans were children?

No, I didn't think Africans were children.

Did I think they were adults?

I thought African adults were adults ...

Let him come into the open, I cried now. Obviously he'd elected me his enemy. I would be glad to know the reason for that. Let him say, clearly, what, clearly, he was thinking: that I was some sort of parasite on African literature, and that my only interest in it was that I was paid to discuss it. I would answer plain charges plainly, if he would make them.

Why was I shaking? he asked. I was shaking, I said, with anger at such sinister obliquity. I was very angry at the sneering indirectness of his attack.

Dear boy, he drawled. I was not, I said, a dear boy. I was not any of these cardboard creatures he was fabricating.

'What are you then?' he cried. 'A dear girl?'

Well, I could not continue, I said. It wasn't possible to do anything on these lines. The shocked studio agreed. Prem said, 'Oh, but let us hear the recording. Play it back, play it back!' If it was too bad, he'd try again.

The curious string of sneers and insinuations was played back.

Oh sorry, sorry, said Prem. Let's do it again. This time it would be useable. He promised. We began again.

And it was exactly as before. The implication that, being interested in writing by and for children, I must believe

195

Africans to be children. Then the question: Why did I do these programmes?—wanting me to squirm and leave money out of the answer. I said it was of course partly for money, but being glad to work for money had never meant that you were without interest in the work: I did the programmes also for the very great pleasure of doing them. I could choose to do other things instead. Whereupon he asked me if I thought I could live by bread alone ... I held on to my fast-failing coolness. It was a case of ... as Dr Johnson said—Oh, said Prem: *do* tell me what Dr Johnson said. I learn *so much* at your feet!

And I walked out.

But I saw, setting aside my fury at the insults and my distress at being understood in terms of so many crude stereotypes ... I saw that the crooked occasion contained a crooked truth. In relation to African writing I *had* been a paternalistic figure, necessarily guilty of patronage, and my genuine interest in the literature, and my real admiration and affection for this writer or that, made things no better.

Jenny now showed me the edition of *Turningpoint* in which, as an interviewer of African writers, I was portrayed as Edward Unblushing, given to cries of 'Exciting! This is *awfully* exciting!' and to applauding the claims of my interviewee to have abandoned rhyme, metre and sense. It was a spoof, said the editorial introduction, on Westernised African writers and their Western flatterers, and offered 'amusing and slightly disturbing reading.'

Well, behind it I was able to trace a whole network of dislikes, more of them being of people than of principles or practices: some being dislikes of persons other than myself, I being a kind of reflector for them all.

The term for much of it was probably ill-will. But the personal roots of the attack hardly affected the real implications. It seemed to me that I perfectly deserved to be misunderstood. I deserved to be seen as a patronising hack. A literature had to get under way in its own awkward fashion, following its own nose. The noses of outsiders were the wrong sorts of noses, altogether.

I'd been part of an odd accident—that, in the absence of outlets at home, Africans had sought publication in the metropolitan centres. So the writing had come from London, New York, Paris. The African in the spoof spent a few reluctant days at home: otherwise he was a happy expatriate, making the rounds of the Western universities. Of course, there was a tendency which the spoof (what an odd word!) had inflated into general practice. I thought of that majority of African writers who'd accepted the never completely disinterested hospitality of the West, without ever becoming this sort of cynical exile. I thought of all the writers who'd figured in my programme: as contributors, as practising writers being interviewed. I couldn't think of one of them whom it was possible to suspect of disdain for the platform offered by the BBC. Oh well, of course some, no doubt, had a sulkiness at the back of the mind, because it was ... a matter of the outsider's nose. But no one refused to make use of the platform. And many had a candid gratitude for it. Well, you had to be a curiously limited person to think of it as wholly an externality, something remorselessly *outside*. The programme was often a piece of Africa, afloat. And no one today, anyway, remains always moored.

I'd been very pleased, I realised, to be a plank in the platform. I strutted about a little, inside myself, because I worked in this corner of the BBC.

But it was a situation where it was best cheerfully to concede that you couldn't win. Quite rightly, you couldn't win. In the end, you were the outsider, and the point must come when you were rejected.

I'd been rejected in a rather foolish way, I thought, by Prem and the author of the spoof—not himself, as it happened, an African. When I was able to detach myself, I was amused by an echo. It was like the infuriating sorts of injustice of which you were likely to be a victim in early years at school. Suddenly they took against you ... and it wasn't that that hurt: it was the fact that their hostility was based on false premises. They'd got you wrong. You could give them a far more accurate account of your failings, and of the reasons why you should be taken to a far corner of the playground and bounced up and down.

I suppose I really wished the African scene had rejected me in some ceremony, followed by a dignified act of execution. Failing that, I'd have liked to have written the spoof myself.

5

It could not, alas, remain gentle between me and my father. He was soon re-inventing us: and, for his attack on the monsters that resulted, using the same weapon as Prem's. That is, insinuation. Nothing ever in the open.

Our son Tom, cheerful student, occupying our house in our absence on holiday while he embarked on some remarkable programme uniting the utmost idleness with the greatest possible intellectual industry, went on a visit to New Chilton. Part of his good-humour and general well-being rested on the cultivation of cadaverousness and ... well, of *un*cultivation in the matter of dress. In the style of the time, he wore, or allowed loosely to cover him, rejected rejects and discarded discards. He sat with the fondest intentions in my father's presence and was entertained with scurrilous attacks on his mother, Kate, and her father, poor dead Jim. It was something about my father that I'd never understand: how he could believe that a plainly devoted son would enjoy attacks on his mother, or on a grandfather with whom he'd had quite a famous affinity. 'I said Jim was a *very* nice man,' said Tom, 'and I thought your dad was going to burst. His face turned terribly red.' Tom had had to say at last that he didn't want to hear this sort of talk. 'He has nothing to stand on now it's come to the end,' he said, 'and so he's hitting out at everyone.' Of course, he added, it was easier for him, Tom, than for us. He had less at stake.

But despite what was at stake—the maintenance of a relationship that couldn't be unimportant, and of simple access to my mother—I wondered now whether I wasn't losing the energy needed to continue ... oh, it was a *pretence,* surely, of a connection. How could I avoid an eleventh hour row of a monumental kind?

198

I couldn't. For now my father wrote about Tom's visit.

'It was good,' said the letter, 'to have Thomas. Such a delightful chap and apparently quite happy, but he does look so unkempt and uncared for. We enjoyed watching him dispose of some nicely prepared meals including a large juicy steak and a glass of beer for his lunch. Before he left for home he had a nice glass of whisky and ginger ale. We were sad to think of him going home to an empty house and his gran acquired further depression as a consequence.'

Plain insinuation: we cared nothing for Tom's welfare, had absolutely no notion that he might be hungry, abandoned him to his own resources while, in decadent Cornwall, we lived the brittle, hollow lives of indifferent parents.

It angered us, on the straightforward grounds that we deeply loved our son, and had the greatest possible respect for his desire to be alone: or, as it sometimes seemed, to be host to a rather large number of friends all with the same wish for solitude.

But my father hadn't, of course, finished. If we were down, my sister was inevitably up. So the portrait of my mother as one made wretched by the spectacle of a grossly neglected grandson continued:

'She was, however, her usual cheery self' (Implication: we'd made my mother desperately unhappy) 'by the time Betty and her family arrived last Sunday. As usual they came early' (Implication: we always came late) 'and we were able to have a pleasant natter over cups of coffee.' (Multiple implication: we never made pleasant natters possible, and somehow never inspired the offer of cups of coffee.) 'Later Brian took me to the Beach Hotel' (Implication: *not* the Marine View, where on his own advice I'd taken my father when he was willing to go; which, since it meant defying the breezes from the sea, was rarely) 'for some drinks. I always like these breaks with Brian and enjoy a pint or two ...' (Implication: if I ever took him to the wrong hotel, I made the enjoyment of a mere pint, never two, very difficult.)

It was not possible to write a bland letter ignoring these complex unpleasantnesses. I wrote to say that whatever game this was, I had no intention of playing it. He meant that we neglected Tom, and were dismal visitors. I should be grateful

199

if he'd write what he meant, so that a direct reply might be made to direct charges.

There was a long silence. I was surprised by the sadness this caused me: absurdly, I now wanted to help him to write a reply.

It came at last:

'We have for years suspected that you deliberately search our letters for any trace of double meanings.' (It sounded extraordinarily like an industry: we'd had this team of inspectors, subjecting my father's epistolary language to every conceivable test.) 'Reading between the lines is not a very profitable exercise—it's peeping through the keyhole—one sees only what one wants to see.

'Of course, neither of you mix a lot.' (Where did that fantasy of shy isolated lives for Kate and me come from?) 'Ted has never known the hurly-burly of an office or of commercial life. Then again you've never been people to entertain'. (In direct contrast to my father, whose house was always brimming with welcome guests.) 'But even so that should be no reason to miss the humorous side of things. I dare not tell you the story of what the leeks said to the white sauce.

'We hope you are well—just keep well, sleep well and hide those livers where they can't be seen.'

I rang my sister, nervously favoured as she'd never been before, and we exchanged hopeless sighs and despairs.

It took months to repair that damage; it was done, and a precarious amity existed, when, on the morning of a planned visit, I woke up with the flu. That's to say, I had that feeling of having been surreptitiously flogged during the night, and had the sorest of throats; so, most displeased with whatever fate it is that distributes flus, rang my father. More for their sakes than for mine I couldn't come with the flu. Oh, he said, he thought it was probably wise of me not to come. The weather bulletins promised rather a bad day. Implication: we were simply anxious to avoid an uncomfortable excursion. 'But,' I cried, 'I'm not thinking of myself, I'm thinking of you. You mustn't be exposed to the flu.' He refused to say the pleasant thing I thought any half-pleasant parent might say: 'Sorry about that—never mind. And of course, you're right—we don't at our ages want to take the risk of catching anything like that.' Instead, his fury accelerated. 'Oh, that's all right,' he said. 'Your mother and I have given up expecting you to come. We've given up caring.' He was using his most abominable voice: like that of someone reluctantly addressing a congress of skunks. I said, very small, 'I see.' And then, 'You've made me feel rather worse. Thank you.' And then I was swept by a fury that was only partly a product of the flu, slammed down the phone and, in all the astonishment of tears, went back to bed.

It took many months to repair *that* damage.

And I wondered, over those months and during the frail armistice that followed, what made him so bitterly uncomfortable a human being. Really, I was the son of a human scorpion! Kate said it must be a chemical matter. You had a certain irritant in your make-up, and you had to behave irritably. As simple as that, perhaps, said Kate, who'd been as deeply stung as any of my father's victims.

He himself had provided over the years a number of tentative explanations. Sometimes with strange candour. In other members of the family, he said once, he could detect the cruel streak that was in him. And, not disapprovingly, he'd more than once referred to himself as a bugger. 'Amazing all the people who think I'm a rotten bugger!' The fact was that very often the simple idea of being a bugger gave him great pleasure. I often thought that in some moods he'd have been glad to have the word inscribed on his tombstone, if he was ever in line for one.

Of course, he had a deep hatred of that surprising insult, old age. He once said fiercely to my harmless sister, 'I hope you grow old so you can see what it's like.' And he added, on what was clearly to him a closely related tack, 'There's not enough tolerance in the world.' And my mother, trusting to his defects of hearing, cried, 'Well, you just go and get some, mate!'

Once he turned to Tom, our son, and said with a kind of jocular anxiety, 'I'm not a hard man, am I? Do you think I'm a hard man?' Tom, not feeling that he was called upon to be that sort of doomsday judge, answered him with a grin and a shrug.

Perhaps it was the only answer.

Epilogue

The first thing we saw, entering the crematorium, was the tall chimney, black smoke welling from it. Because there was so much plastic in coffins, now, an undertaker told me when later I asked about the thick brutal blackness of that smoke. My father would have been furious. 'Should have thought they could do better than that.' But he'd have liked the grounds ... those trim flowerbeds, the neat paths. 'Wonder how many men they employ to look after it?'

Well, he was in that box, then, such a raw-looking box for all its rapid polish. 'Now I know what I shall look like in my coffin.' The priest was a small, young, hurried man. 'Our dearly beloved brother, Ernest ...' *Ernest!* How he would have bridled at the error. Though he would have expected it, of course. As with cinema ushers and bus conductors, so with parsons: they were in serious need of being reported to their superiors.

My mother shaking at my side. Suddenly she was all tears. She was nothing but tears. The service, allowed to become this hasty banality, scurried to its end: and I then became aware that the coffin was sinking.

It was not rolling forward, as in the other crematorium services I'd attended. With complete indifference to one of the most pervasive of man's notions of destination, it had been arranged that the coffin should go down.

But how he would have raged at *that!* At the ineptitude of it! Going *down!*

And down, absurdly, relentlessly, my poor father—deprived of all means of protest—went.